# Fists of Fury

# Bruce Lee

## By Edward Gross

PIONEER BOOKS, INC.        LAS VEGAS, NEVADA

# Designed and Edited by Hal Schuster
## with assistance from James R. Martin

**EDWARD GROSS** has written for a variety of publications, including PREMIERE, STARLOG, COMICS SCENE, NEW YORK/LONG ISLAND NIGHTLIFE, FANGORIA and CINEFANTASTIQUE. He is the author of TREK: THE LOST YEARS, THE UNOFFICIAL TALE OF BEAUTY AND THE BEAST, THE MAKING OF THE NEXT GENERATION, THE ODD COUPLE COMPANION, SECRET FILE: THE MAKING OF A WISEGUY and PAUL McCARTNEY: 20 YEARS ON HIS OWN. In addition, he co-authored the story for an episode of ABC's SUPERCARRIER and his first screenplay is scheduled to go into production later this year. He lives on Long Island, New York with his wife Eileen and their son, Teddy.

**Library of Congress Cataloging-in-Publication Data**
Edward Gross, 1960—
    Bruce Lee: Fists of Fury

  1.   Bruce Lee: Fists of Fury  (biography)
 I. Title

Copyright (c) 1990 by Pioneer Books, Inc. All rights reserved.
All artwork copyright (c) 1990 Pioneer Books, Inc. All illustrations are used to illustrate reviews only and are in no way intended to infringe on characters or concepts of any party. All rights reserved.
Published by Pioneer Books, Inc., 5715 N. Balsam Rd., Las Vegas, NV, 89130.

First Printing, 1990

**To my father who encouraged me to try....now I do**

**ACKNOWLEDGEMENTS:** Special thanks in making this book a reality to Robert Clouse, Richard Moore, Stuart at Book City Collectables, Steven Flynn for access to his pressbook files; Chuck Norris, for talking about these films indepth with me and, as always, my wife, Eileen who has had to deal with kung fu films everytime she walked into the living room.

**AUTHOR'S NOTE:** The titles used in this book are based on the U.S. releases. Our **Fists of Fury** was originally entitled **The Big Boss** when released in Hong Kong, while our **The Chinese Connection** had been called **Fists of Fury**. In addition, **Return of the Dragon**, which was sold as a sequel to **Enter the Dragon** in America, was actually filmed prior to that movie and released in Hong Kong as **Way of the Dragon**. **Enter the Dragon** and **Game of Death** had the same titles both here and abroad.

| Page | Description |
|---|---|
| **6** | an introduction and explanation from the author as to why he wanted to write a book about Bruce Lee |
| **8** | a brief biography of Bruce Lee and the troubled path which ultimately led to movie stardom |
| **20** | the Green Hornet, launched in the wake of Batman, launched Bruce Lee's karate mastery into the public eye |
| **42** | Fists of Fury made on a small budget in Hong Kong, earned a cult following and began a new trend of martial arts films |
| **62** | The Chinese Connection, which was called Fists of Fury in the Orient, transcended the genre to appeal to a larger audience |
| **82** | Return of the Dragon, the first film Bruce Lee wrote and directed, was actually made before Enter the Dragon and originally entitled Way of the Dragon |
| **100** | Enter the Dragon brought Bruce Lee to America where he introduced higher production values into martial arts film-making |
| **126** | Game of Death proved all to prophetic as Bruce Lee died before the film entered theaters and little of his fabulous work appears on the screen |
| **146** | Bruce Lee, taken from his many fans too soon, left many imitators to try to fill the void he left (—see also special section at end of book) |
| **152** | The Silent Flute, also known as Circle of Iron, was the film Bruce Lee almost made |

**FISTS OF FURY: THE FILMS OF BRUCE LEE**

# INTRODUCTION

My father was knocked out by Bruce Lee.
It was the early 1960's and Bruce Lee was giving a demonstration at a karate tournament. My father, a 10th degree black belt, got on stage to partake in free-fighting. They bowed to each other and my father raised his hands.
"I woke up twenty minutes later," he muses, a victim of Lee's lighting fast legs.
Why, you may wonder, would somebody brag about something like that? Hey, how many kids can claim that their father was knocked out by someone like Bruce Lee? In a way it's kind of nice to be able to tap into the Bruce Lee phenomenon, even in so unorthodox a manner.
It is that phenomenon which will be explored in **Fists of Fury: The Films of Bruce Lee**. A biography of Lee will be followed by a complete guide to his television work on **The Green Hornet** and **Longstreet**, and then a complete analysis of the movies **Fists of Fury, The Chinese Connection, Return of the Dragon, Enter the Dragon** and **Game of Death**. In addition, the text examines **Circle of Iron**, the film based on Lee's **The Silent Flute**, and presents the information contained in the original theatrical pressbooks for each of his motion pictures.
The production companies continually made note that Lee was American-born, as though they felt they needed to do so in order to protect the film.
Since his death in 1973, the legend of Bruce Lee has continued to grow. This book is designed to serve as an overview of his career and a tribute to his memory.

—Edward Gross
February, 1990

# A Brief Biography

Being all that he could be.

Sounding like an ad for the U.S. Army, it epitomizes the philosophy driving Bruce Lee's life and career as a martial artist and film-maker. He possessed a strength of character powerful enough to conquer the adversities life threw at him and channel them into a phenomenon that elevated him to the status of cultural icon.

Cultural icons are a fascinating lot, transcending their own lifetimes and achieving immortality in death. They touch the spirit of one generation after another, always remaining larger than life, a symbol; an ideal to strive towards and an intangible fantasy image or remembrance of a greater than real past.

John Wayne carries the image of the Old West coupled with patriotism; James Dean, the eternal rebel without a cause. Marilyn Monroe remains every man's fantasy of a beautiful blonde Hollywood goddess while Elvis Presley will always be the King of Rock 'n' Roll. John Lennon, cut down by a fan's bullets resurrects sounds of the Sixties, part of a musical tradition unlike any the world will ever see again. And Bruce Lee is still the philosopher and martial artist supreme, offering his followers a higher level of existence to struggle towards, larger in death than in life. He is the ultimate man of action.

Bruce Lee was born Lee Jun Fan on November 27, 1940. He would not be known as Bruce Lee until many years later. Some sources claim 1940 as the year of the dragon, thus giving birth to his nickname, "The Little Dragon." Other sources proclaim he was bestowed that title as a child actor in Hong Kong.

The city of his birth was San Francisco, where his parents temporarily resided at the time. His father was on tour with the Cantonese Opera Company of Hong Kong. Although the family returned home little more than three months later, Lee had already "cameoed" in his first feature film, **Golden Gate Girl**. One could easily argue that his destiny to become an actor was set at that young age.

At six he was featured in **The Beginning of a Boy,** and then co-starred with his father in the comedy **My Son A-Chung**. By 1958 he had already starred in 20 films, nearly all of which cast him as a rebel/juvenile delinquent in the mode of *The Blackboard Jungle*. This period culminated in two films which represented the dual nature of Bruce Lee.

In **The Orphan** he played a street-wise punk involved in an unending number of fights. Counterpointing this combative role, **The Thunderstorm**, featured no fight scenes at all. In fact, he portrayed a character who refused to fight, regardless of the provocation. This latter characterization first showcased the persona he would adopt for **Fists of Fury**. That film, while beginning the same as **The Thunderstorm**, would take a dramatic turn at midpoint as he unleased his power and exploded into action. The film made use of the traditional metaphor in which the hero, finally provoked beyond the point of endurance, finally faces his oppressor and defeats it.

The authors of *From Bruce Lee to the Ninjas* (Citadel Books) wrote, "Even at the age of seven, Lee's screen persona was strong. He was a clever, capable, but short-tempered little ruffian who specialized in the scowl, the pout, the stare and the slow burn. This character served him on the streets as well. Ignoring the lessons of his films and his family, Bruce Lee, in his own words, 'went looking for a fight.'"

By his late teens there were two options open for Lee: stardom or the dark path of back alleys and dank jail cells. At first it seemed as if the latter would surely prove the stronger magnet and win out. Lee caused trouble wherever he went, aided in no small part by the gang he travelled with. This, ironically enough, led him to study kung fu, which he first saw as a means of making himself a more deadly fighting machine. It would be other aspects of the ancient art and philosophy that would bring the greatest changes in his life.

"Kids in [Hong Kong] having nothing to look forward to," he'd explained to the press. "The white kids [British] have all the best jobs and the rest of us had to work for them. That's why most of the kids became punks. Life in Hong Kong is so bad. Kids in slums can never get out. *I* always fought with my gang behind me. In school, our favorite weapons were the chains we'd find in the 'cans'. Those days, kids improvised all kinds of weapons—even shoes with razors attached. I only took kung fu when I began to feel insecure. I kept wondering what would happen to me if my gang was not around when I met a rival gang.

"[The gangs] didn't take kung fu for health reasons, just to learn to fight," he elaborated elsewhere. "Like old tradition, one school would challenge another and a designated place and time would be set. On the day of reckoning, both schools would have their instructors and students to cheer their fighter. Impromptu rules would be established, but those rules would be so minimal that the fight would be just about 'all out'. Nobody really got hurt because the arts weren't that effective. Those guys would have torn shirts and bloody noses, but I never saw anybody really get hurt badly enough to be sent to the hospital."

Even as this disreputable aspect of Lee grew, so did he become more and more popular as a film star.. His success only served to make him yet more defiant of authority.

In 1979, *Inside Kung Fu* magazine reported, "Run Run Shaw, an extremely popular producer, wanted to sign Bruce to star in movies for him. It was then that Bruce, who never really liked school, announced to his mother that he wanted to quit high school and accept Shaw's offer. He felt certain that he could become a star. Grace also believed he could be successful, but was deeply concerned about what was happening to him. For one thing, he was becoming more and more involved in street fighting. Also, she felt it was very important for him to finish high school and get his diploma. The situation finally came to a head when Bruce was picked up by the police for fighting. For Grace, this was the final straw. She didn't want him to accept Shaw's offer and in 1959 sent him to live with friends in the United States where he would finish high school. She knew in her heart that this would be his only chance to straighten out and make something of his life, and she was right. Bruce finished high school and went to college in Washington."

The high school was Seattle's Edison, where Lee earned money giving dance lessons (something he had excelled at in Hong Kong) and waiting tables. After graduating, he went on to attend the University of Washington majoring in philosophy. He would also develop more fully as a martial artist, gaining a determination to be the *best*. What had started as a way of protecting himself in street fighting, suddenly became a way of life. Lee became so proficient a martial artist that he earned spending money by teaching kung fu to his fellow students.

In that way he eventually met his wife, Linda Emery. They eventually had two children.

In college Lee wrote a thesis on kung fu, in which, according to Linda Lee and Tom Bleecker's *The Bruce Lee Story,* Lee himself noted, "About four years of hard training in the art of gung fu [the Catonese phrase for kung fu], I began to understand and felt the principle of gentleness—the art of neutralizing one's energy. All these must be done in calmness and without striving. It sounded sim-

ple, but in actual application it was difficult."

That difficulty arose when he went up against an opponent, and after a number of kicks and punches had been exchanged, he became more determined to be victorious in the struggle. The turning point for him was when his professor, Yip Man—the head of the Wing Chun School, came up to him and told him to relax, to forget about himself and follow his opponent's movement. He must learn to let his mind, the basic reality, countermove without interfering deliberation. Most importantly, he had to learn "the art of detachment." At that moment, Lee finally realized that he must relax and release the pent up tension he had carried from his years on the streets of Hong Kong, but that command to himself was already self-defeating. His instructor would then tell him never to assert himself against nature; to "never be in frontal opposition to any problem, but control it by swinging with it."

Lee's instructor said he should go home and relax by taking several weeks off. At this fateful juncture Lee would would undertake a seemingly ordinary action that would bring him to a moment of catharsis that would forever change his life.

"I gave up and went sailing alone in a junk," the text detailed Lee saying. "On the sea, I thought of all my past training and got mad at myself and punched at the water. Right then at that moment, a thought suddenly struck me. Wasn't this water, the very basic stuff, the essence of gung fu? Didn't the common water just illustrate to me the principle of gung fu? I struck it just now, but it did not suffer hurt. Again I stabbed it with all my might, yet it was not wounded. I then tried to grasp a handful of it but it was impossible. This water, the softest substance in the world, could fit into any container. Although it seemed weak, it could penetrate the hardest substance in the world. That was it! I wanted to be like the nature of water.

"Suddenly a bird flew past and cast its reflection on the water. Right then, as I was absorbing myself, another mystic sense of hidden meaning started upon me. Shouldn't it be the same then that the thoughts and emotions I had in front of an opponent passed like the reflection of the bird over the water? This was exactly what Professor Yip Man meant by being detached—not being without emotion or feeling, but being one in whom feeling was not sticky or blocked. Therefore, in order to control myself I must first accept myself by going with, and not against, my nature. I lay on the boat and felt that I had united with Tao; I had become one with nature. I just lay there and let the boat drift freely and irresistibly according to its own will. For at that moment I had achieved a state of inner feeling in which opposition had become mutually cooperative instead of mutually exclusive, in which there was no longer any conflict in my mind. The whole world to me was unitary."

Lee continued to develop his skills, and ultimately created his own form of the martial arts known as jeet kune do, which essentially means "The Way of the Intercepting Fist."

"I hate to label any fighting into a style," he had explained. "Fighting should not be stylized. When you fight, you should prepare to handle yourself against any kind of opponent, whether he is a boxer, judoist or wrestler. You see, many people who come to instruction say, 'Like man, like what is the truth? Hand it over to me.' So therefore one guy would say, 'I'll give you the Chinese way of doing it.' In jeet kune do, unless they are men with three hands or men with four legs, then there are different ways of doing it. If you have only two hands and two legs, nationalities don't mean anything. We must approach it as an expression of oneself. When you go to a Japanese style, you are expressing a Japanese style. You are not expressing yourself. Basically, my style uses more footwork than the more elementary style. It is an art, and like any art the martial arts are ultimately self-knowledge. A punch or kick is not to knock the hell out of the guy in front of you, but to knock the hell out of your ego, your fear, or your hang-ups. Once that is clear, you can express yourself clearly."

Word of Lee's philosophy spread quickly, and as many came to him he was able to open three jeet kune do schools. Lee kept himself alive financially by teaching private lessons to celebrities, among them basketball great Kareem Abdul-Jabbar and actors Steve McQueen and James Coburn. The latter had recently come off of his *Our Man Flint* and *In Like Flint* films, in which he had utilized karate. Coburn and Lee meshed well together and developed a long-standing friendship.

Despite his success in the world of martial arts, Lee still wanted to break into films. Unfortunately Lee the teacher was far more successful than Lee the actor, despite his success in this field of endeavor a decade before. Offers were not quick in coming. While he would eventually play the role of Kato for **The Green Hornet** television series and in a little other episodic work, Hollywood somehow refused to take serious notice of him.

Lee's determination crystallized during a period when he was laid up for several weeks after injuring his back.

"I never wanted a job in an office or any job that I had to work eight hours a day at—day in and day out," Lee had stated. "I don't think I could have stood it...[But as I lay there], I was determined then to be an actor. Not just an actor, but a star."

Jaded by the Hollywood process, Lee and his family packed up and moved back to Hong Kong. There he discovered his destiny!

# TV Lee

*Batman* was 1989's number one grossing motion picture. A variety of super hero films will reach theatres throughout the early 1990s hoping to find their own success by riding the crest of the wave begun by the popular film. This exactly replays events from the 1960s. A similar hope first brought Bruce Lee to American television screens.

In 1966, producer William Dozier and 20th Century Fox arranged for the Caped Crusader to appear on the ABC television network to great success. *Batman*, with its tongue-in-cheek approach and vast array of guest villains, spawned a variety of prime time super heroes, including *Mr. Terrific*, *Captain Nice* and **The Green Hornet**. While the first two imitated Batman's campy style, **The Green Hornet** instead, tried to carve out its own territory by playing it straight. The series teamed Brit Reid, a.k.a. the Green Hornet, and Kato in action-filled adventures pitting them against the legions of organized crime. The earlier *Batman* television series had become famous for its devotion to gadgets, ranging from special planes to unique boomerangs and distinctive cars. The Green Hornet and Kato had their own version of the Batmobile, called The Black Beauty, which contained a number of "extras" that would have made James Bond proud.

Now, some twenty four years later, **The Green Hornet** is remembered primarily for featuring Bruce Lee as Kato, side-kick to the Hornet. When the television series was first promoted, the Green Hornet, as the title character, was the star. Yet when the movies of the series would later be released and in all history books since, the emphasis has firmly shifted to Kato. This series earned the distinction of being one of the vehicles that launched the martial arts sensation into the national spotlight earning practitioners of Oriental fighting systems superstar status.

"The only reason I ever got that job was because I was the only Chinaman in all California who could pronounce Brit

Reid," Lee mused during the sixties. "Maybe when I was hired to play Kato in **The Green Hornet** it was an accident. I didn't have any [American] acting experience. I was [originally] offered a number one-spot in a proposed one-hour series titled *Number One Son*, and it was going to be like a Chinese James Bond-type of thing. I wanted to make sure before I signed that there wouldn't be any 'ah-so's' and 'chop-chops' in the dialogue and that I would not be required to go bouncing around with a pigtail. While attending a 'quickie' one month private course in acting, the producer changed his mind and decided that I would be Kato instead."

"Bruce has one of the finest natural acting talents that I have ever seen in my years in the industry," said William Dozier. "He is a handsome young man and fits the role of Kato perfectly. His ability as a natural athlete provides a good foundation for the role of Kato, who often steps in to save the Green Hornet when they are battling criminals."

Bruce Lee lit up screens across the country delivering an incredible Kato, bringing a sense of realism to the fight scenes quite unlike those of any show then on the air. "One of the main characteristics of the show will be the the speed of the fights and the simplicity in finishing off the Hornet's enemies," said Lee.

Apparently the "speed" was too much, as **The Green Hornet** lasted only 26 episodes, plus a two-part stint on *Batman* in which the duo came up first against Batman and Robin and then, ultimately, faced Colonel Gumm.

The October, 1979 edition of *Fighting Stars* magazine presented the following account of Lee's visit to the realm of the Dark Knight:

"As long as both shows were so popular among viewers, a Kato-Robin confrontation was unavoidable. The young public was clamoring for one. 'The director decided we

should participate in the *Batman* series instead of ours,' Bruce Lee said. He had no idea what the director had in mind, but after reading the script, he grinned and said to himself, 'This is great. Kato finally gets to fight Robin.'

"Bruce was a great kidder. He relished playing jokes. Especially on someone he did not care for. On the day Kato was to fight Robin, Bruce put on his most solemn face. He walked around as though carrying a heavy burden on his shoulders. He hardly said anything and did not kid around with the crew in his usual manner. He was not the same Bruce Lee everyone knew.

"On the *Batman* set Bruce continued his pretense. He stood in a fighting stance, teeth clenched and eyes squinted behind Kato's mask. Meanwhile, Ward as Robin, stood a good distance away from him and attempted to calm him with irrelevant comments which Bruce just ignored. Finally, the director ordered them to proceed and the camera began to roll. Bruce held his deadpan expression and inched his way toward his opponent. Ward kept his distance and yelled, 'Bruce, remember this is not for real. It's just a show!'

"Bruce later related the incident. 'I had a hard time keeping a straight face,' he said. 'I started to crowd Burt and he began to flap his elbows and jump around me. I was really keeping him scared and I hear someone in the back whisper, "The black panther and the yellow chicken," At that point, I burst out laughing. I just couldn't keep a straight face anymore.'

"The director didn't want to upset any fans, so he cleverly let the heroes fight to a draw. Bruce viewed the whole event with amusement. 'Lucky for Robin that it was not for real; otherwise he would have been one dead bird.'"

Van Williams, who portrayed Brit Reid/The Green Hornet, noted in the pages of *Black Belt* magazine, "I felt Bruce was kind of in the wrong place there in **The Green Hornet**. The stuff that he did in the series was probably the most popular part of the show—the action sequences doing his gung fu and the fight scenes we did. He got quite a following out of that—a worldwide following. I felt it was just a matter of time. That's the irony of the thing. It is still one of the gripes I've got about the business as it is nowadays: you still have to go abroad to become a star. Nobody could really see what this guy had to offer as far as worldwide popularity is concerned. He had to go abroad, but the Asians finally saw what he had—primarily, I think, through **The Green Hornet** series because it ran in Japan and, as far as I know, in Hong Kong as well as other places."

Thanks to episodes of the series being released overseas as feature films, Lee's Kato was quickly catching on, and he soon became aware of his impact.

"After a personal appearance at Madison Square Garden at a karate tournament," Lee reflected, "I started to make an exit, escorted by three karate men. I was practically mobbed as I approached the main lobby, and I had to make a hasty exit through a side door. In Fresno, California I was scratched, kicked and gouged by riotous fans. I just couldn't protect myself without doing bodily harm to my fans, whose aim, after all, was not to hurt me.

"I guess I'm the only guy who ventured away from [Hong Kong] and became an actor," he added elsewhere. "To most people, including actors and actresses, Hollywood is like a magic kingdom. It's beyond everyone's reach and when I made it, they thought I'd accomplished an incredible feat. But if my success was based on these two facts alone, then why is it that **The Green Hornet** smashed box offices in Singapore, Philippines and other countries I haven't even visited? Some martial artists are now going to Hong Kong to be in movies. They think they

can be lucky too. Well, I don't believe in pure luck. You have to create your own luck. You have to be aware of the opportunities around you and take advantage of them. Some guys may not believe it, but I spent thousands of hours perfecting whatever I did."

After **The Green Hornet**, Lee made guest appearances in such prime time TV series as Raymond Burr's **Ironside** and **Here Come the Brides**, as well as assaying a small part in the James Garner film, **Marlowe**, which was written and co-produced by Lee student, Stirling Silliphant.

"In any of the films I was writing," Silliphant said in the *Bruce Lee Memorial Book*, "I always tried either to incorporate Bruce as an actor or as a behind-the-scenes stuntman whenever I could. For example, I wrote a film for MGM called **Marlowe** with James Garner. I put two sequences into it—the two best scenes in the film—where Bruce comes into Garner's office and tears it up and another when he meets Garner up on the roof of the Occidental building and goes kicking and screaming off into space. That probably was Bruce's first American feature film appearance."

According to the authors of *From Bruce Lee to the Ninjas: Martial Arts Movies*, Lee also served as a technical advisor on Dean Martin's 1969 Matt Helm romp, *The Wrecking Crew*.

Lee's greatest critical reaction, however, came from what was supposed to be a one-shot appearance in the James Franciscus series, **Longstreet**. The show ran on ABC during the 1970-71 television season. In that series, Franciscus portrayed insurance investigator Mike Longstreet, who, while in the midst of an investigation, was attacked by a group who killed his wife and beat him in such a way as to leave him blind. Naturally this didn't stop him from continuing in his occupation, aided by a seeing eye dog named Pax and the self-defense skills taught to him by Bruce Lee.

In *Black Belt's Bruce Lee Memorial Book*, writer Stirling Silliphant wrote, "I was doing a television show called **Longstreet**. I had sold the series with a 90-minute pilot film. Now the time had come to do the first on-the-air one-hour episode. Together, Bruce and I worked out our opening story. I called it 'The Way of the Intercepting Fist', which was, of course, a literal translation of 'jeet kune do', Bruce's personal martial art. It was a very straightline story in which James Franciscus, the blind detective, is assaulted by some toughs in the beginning and told to keep off the dock. He is saved from being hurt by a Chinese antique dealer—Bruce—who just happens to be walking by and clobbers these guys with kicks and punches. The detective wants to get back at his assailants and asks Bruce what he did and how he did it. But Bruce doesn't want to teach him, because the blind man's motivations for learning is wrong. So the story had to do with teaching Franciscus how to learn the way of the intercepting fist.

"We had more fan mail on that episode than on any other shows we did in the series," he added. "Bruce, in turn, got a tremendous volume of letters and reactions from both critics and viewers. As a matter of fact, it was that episode which gave him, I like to believe, his first good film to show himself off to the world with pride and dignity as an Oriental martial artist. And even though I wrote it, I think it probably was the best martial art film that has ever been on the air. What I did was simply to take many of the things Bruce had taught me and put them into the script. In any event, as a result of that episode, the network and Paramount wanted Bruce in more episodes. Ultimately we used him in three other **Longstreet**s during that year before he went to Hong Kong and rose to superstar status. It was after this first TV episode he was approached by Ted

Ashley of Warner Brothers and by Screen Gems (as well as by Paramount) to sign for a series they hoped to develop for him."

They never did, as motion pictures had begun their siren call beckoning Bruce Lee on to his true destiny.

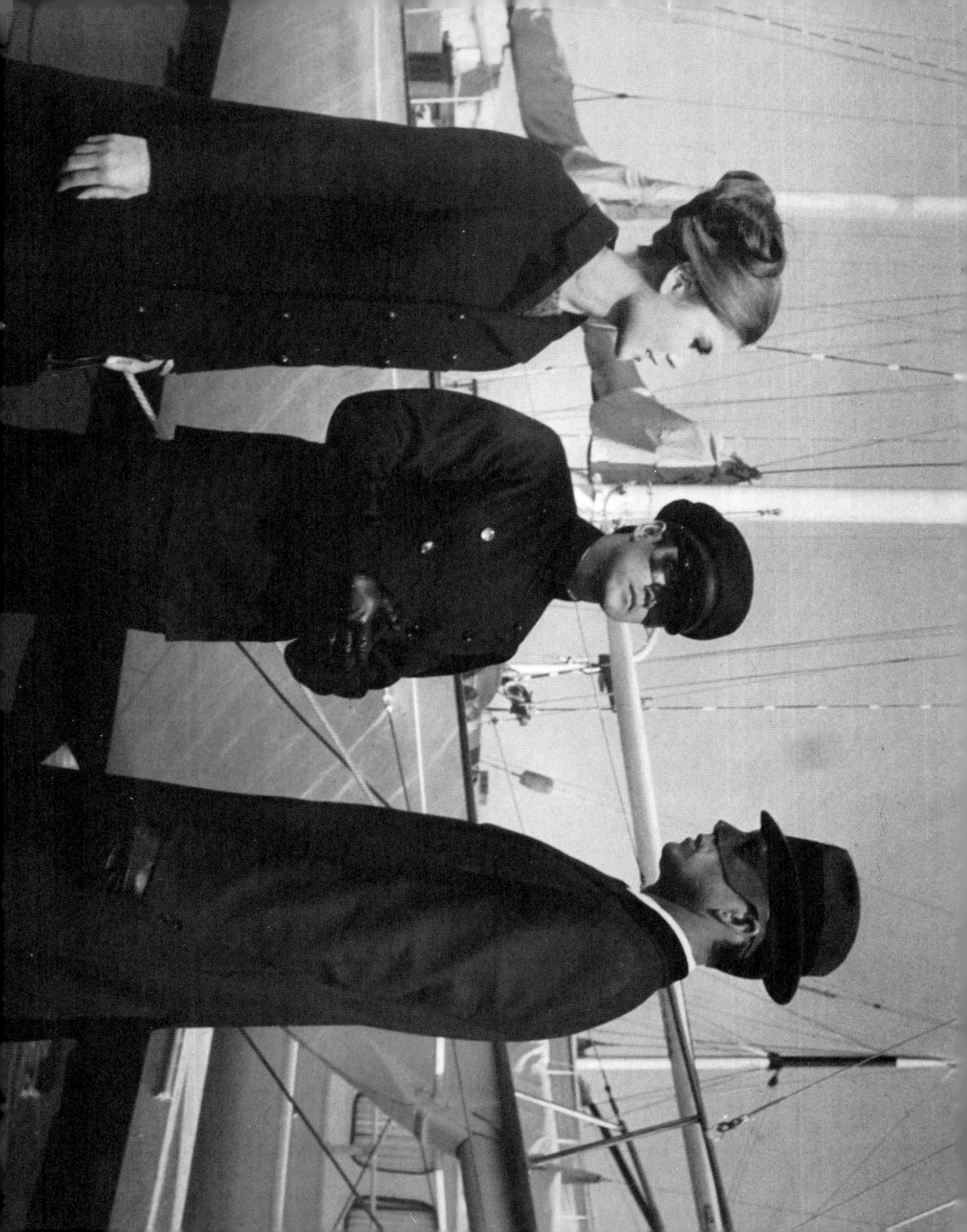

# EPISODE GUIDE TO THE GREEN HORNET

EPISODE 1: "THE SILENT GUN"
Written by Ken Pettus
Directed by Leslie H. Martinson
Guest Starring: Lloyd Bochner, Henry Evans, Charlies Francisco, Kelly Jean Peters, Ed McGrealy, Max Klevin, Al McGranary, Breland Rice and Bob Harvey
When Dave Bannister is murdered at his father's funeral, the Green Hornet and Kato get involved. They find the root cause of the violent action, lust for possession of a weapon known as the "silent gun", which Bannister's father had developed. The gun works ideally as a weapon for a killer; it fires without a flash or sound.
Upon further investigation they learn that Dave Bannister had stolen the gun from his father to pay off gambling debts owed to a man named Trump. He in turn had Dave's father killed when the man discovered this and threatened to go to the police. Dave was murdered when he became suspicious of Trump.
The Hornet and Kato manage to apprehend Trump, but not before nearly being killed in the process.

EPISODE 2: "GIVE 'EM ENOUGH ROPE"
Written by Gwen Bagni and Paul Dubov
Directed by Seymour Robbie
Guest Starring: Diana Hyland, Mort Mills, Jerry Ayers, David Renard, Joe Sirola and Ken Strange
The Green Hornet and Kato come up against the Man in Black, who is responsible for a strangulation murder. The duo are fearful that this is a serial killer they are pursuing, but it turns out to be a supposed accident victim out to defraud his insurance company for a large sum of money.

EPISODE 3: "PROGRAMMED FOR DEATH"
Written by Jerry Thomas, Story by Lewis Reed
Directed by Larry Peerce
Guest Starring: Signe Hasso, Richard Cutting, Normal Leavitt, Pat Tidy, Barbara Badcock, Gary Owens, Sheila Leighton, Don Eitner and John Alvar
Diamond counterfeiters realize that a reporter has discovered their crimes. He is killed before he can write his story, murdered by a leopard attracted by a transmitter secreted in his clothing. The murder by proxy leaves enough clues for Brit Reid to find, and an investigation by the Green Hornet and Kato is triggered. And, of course, meeting the requirements of television crime fiction, the investigation leads to the demise of the counterfeiting operation.

EPISODE 4: "CRIME WAVE"
Written by Sheldon Stark
Directed by Larry Peerce
Guest Starring: Peter Haskell, Sheila Wells, Denny Costello, Jennifer Stuart, Ron Burke, Gary Owens, Wayne Sutherlin, Jack Garner, Ken Strange and Dee Sutherlin
When diamond thieves implicate the Green Hornet in an intricate diamond robbery on a boarding airplane, it is up to the Hornet and Kato to clear his name.

# Fists Of Fury

**EPISODE 5: "THE FROG IS A DEADLY WEAPON"**
*Written by William L. Stuart*
*Directed by Leslie H. Martinson*
*Guest Starring: Victor Jory, Nedra Vallen, Barbara Babcock, Geroge Robotham, Rudy Hansen and Roger Heldfond*
A gangster is supposedly dead. Then fisherman Nat Pyle offers to sell proof of the his continued existence to Brit Reid. Before he can do so, he is slain, sending the Green Hornet and Kato in grim pursuit of the truth. What they ultimately discover is that the gangster has undergone plastic surgery and and adopted the role of a Howard Hughes-type of recluse millionaire. Now he will allow *nothing* to get in the way of his new life. Once they discover his real identity, the Hornet and Kato don't leave the former gangster much of a choice in the matter.

**EPISODE 6: "EAT, DRINK AND BE DEAD"**
*Written by Richard Landau*
*Directed by Murray Golden*
*Guest Starring: Jason Evers, Harry Lauter, Harry Fleer, William McLennan, Eddie Ness, Shep Sanders and Jo Ann Milam*
This episode has a very simple plot. The Green Hornet and Kato use every means at their disposal to take down a dairy. The dairy is not as innocent as it appears but is actually the front for a bootlegging operation.

**EPISODE 7: "BEAUTIFUL DREAM", PART ONE**
*Written by Ken Pettus and Lorenzo Semple, Jr.*
*Directed by Allen Reisner*
*Guest Starring: Goffrey Horne, Pamela Curran, Henry Hunter, Jean Marie, Victoria George, Maurice Manson, Barbara Gates and Marina Ghane*

**EPISODE 8: "BEAUTIFUL DREAMER", PART TWO**
*Written by Ken Pettus and Lorenzo Semple, Jr.*
*Directed by Allen Reisner*
*Guest Starring: Goffrey Horne, Pamela Curran, Henry Hunter, Jean Marie, Victoria George, Maurice Manson, Barbara Gates, Marina Ghane, Gary Owens, Sandy Kevin, Jerry Catron, Chuck Hicks, Jean-Marie*
The Green Hornet and Kato want to bring down the Vale of Eden Health Club, which actually has a much deadlier agenda than helping people become healthy. They actually brainwash their customers, forcing them to commit crimes. The masterminds behind the club lose nothing if their pawns are caught. Yet they have everything to gain when they succeed. A beautiful no risk situation until the Green Hornet and Kato enter the picture. The first mistake or the men behind the club is to have one of their clients try to eliminate Brit Reid. Their second mistake...actually they don't get the opportunity to make a second mistake.

**EPISODE 9: "THE RAY IS FOR KILLING"**
*Written by Lee Loeb*
*Directed by William Baudine*
*Guest Starring: Robert McQueeney, Bill Baldwin, Bob Gunner, Mike Mahoney and Jim Raymond*
When a million dollars worth of paintings on loan to Brit Reid are stolen, it is up to the Green Hornet and Kato to act on the kidnapper's demands. What they don't expect is for said kidnapper to be armed with a high-powered laser. Needless to say, things turn out okay for our heroes and the kidnapper meets a proper fate.

*EPISODE 10: "THE PREYING MANTIS"*
*Written by Ken Pettus and Charles Hoffman, Story by Charles Hoffman*
*Directed by Norman Foster*
*Guest Starring: Mako, Allen Jung, Tom Drake, Gary Owens, Al Huang, Lang Yun*
Undoubtedly inspired by the newfound status of Bruce Lee and the growing popularity of kung fu, this episode pits our duo against a kung fu gang in Chinatown. The gang works as part of a protection racket, using their mastery of the martial arts in ways which disgrace the philosophy of the venerated forms. This show should have been *the* Kato story of the series, pitting the single master martial artist against the horde of lesser practitioners in the style of the later movies, but, as usual, he was merely the Hornet's sidekick.

*EPISODE 11: "THE HUNTERS AND THE HUNTED"*
*Written by Jerry Thomas*
*Directed by William Baudine*
*Guest Starring: Robert Strauss, Charles Bateman, Douglas Evans, Rand Brooks, Bill Walker, Frank Gerstle, Dick Dial and Gene LeBell*
City gang leaders are being killed by jungle weapons including poison darts and spears. The Green Hornet finds himself at the top of the death list, targeted for destruction. Since the series would not proceed well without the presecne of the title hero, they fail!

*EPISODE 12: "DEADLINE FOR DEATH"*
*Written by Ken Pettus*
*Directed by Richard Bluel*
*Guest Starring: James Best, Lynda Day (George), Jacques Aubuchon, Pat Patterson, Kirby Brumfield, Annazette Williams, Gary Owens, Glen Wilder and Roydon Clark*
Another story that is not too difficult to summarize: the Green Hornet and Kato want to crack a burglary ring led by a beautiful woman. Once again, as all good heroes do in televisionland, they succeed.

*EPISODE 13: "THE SECRET OF THE SALLY BELL"*
*Written by William L. Stuart*
*Directed by Robert L. Friend*
*Guest Starring: Warren Kemmerling, Beth Brickell, Jacques Dendeaux, Greg Benedict, Dave Perna, Ann Rexford, Gary Owens, Timothy Scott and James Farley*
The Green Hornet must avoid an assassin's bullet as he investigates the apparent disappearance of a cargo-load of drugs supposedly in route to be placed aboard the vessel named Sally Bell. In addition, the Green Hornet and Kato must elude various traps set by the drug ring.

*EPISODE 14: "FREEWAY TO DEATH"*
*Written by Ken Pettus*
*Directed by Allen Reisner*
*Guest Starring: Jeffrey Hunter, John Hubbard, David Fresco, Reggie Parton, Harvey Parry and Fred Krone*
The Green Hornet and Kato must destroy a contruction racket which builds inferior and unsafe buildings to protect the city. Of course, they succeed in bringing down the nefarious badguys.

# Fists Of Fury

EPISODE 15: "MAY THE BEST MAN LOSE"
*Written by Judith and Robert Guy Barrows*
*Directed by Allen Reisner*
*Guest Starring: Harold Gould, Linden Childes, Robert Hoy, Troy Melton, Bill Phupps, Stuart Nisset, Gary Owens and Jim Drum*
The aide of a politician is killed in an explosion designed to kill the politician himself. It turns out—as the efforts of the Green Hornet and Kato reveal—to have been the work of his opponent's campaign manager, working to elect his candidate no matter what it might take.

EPISODE 16: "SEEK, STALK AND DESTROY"
*Written by Jerry Thomas*
*Directed by George Waggner*
*Guest Starring: Ralph Meeker, Raymond St. Jacques, Paul Carr, John Baer, Harvey Parry and E.J. Andre*
The Green Hornet and Kato must stop a trio of war veterans who have stolen an army tank to free a comrade from prison. It seems that the man is on death row for killing the group's former general—a crime he is innocent of. The Green Hornet and Kato help justice prevail.

EPISODE 17: "CORPSE OF THE YEAR", PART ONE
*Written by Ken Pettus*
*Directed by James Komack*
*Guest Starring: Joanna Dru, Celia Kaye, J. Edward McKinley, Tom Simcox, Cesare Danova, Barbara Babcock, Nora Marlowe, Jack Garner, Sidney Smith, Sally Mills and Angelique*

EPISODE 18: "CORPSE OF THE YEAR", PART TWO
*Written by Ken Pettus*
*Directed by James Komack*
*Guest Starring Joanna Dru, Celia Kaye, J. Edward McKinley, Tom Simcox, Cesare Danova, Barbara Babcock, Nora Marlowe, Jack Garner, Sidney Smith, Sally Mills and Angelique*
A double of the Green Hornet utilizes an exact copy of the Black Beauty to kill his victims. It is up to the real McCoy to put an end to the impersonator and clear himself of the crimes.

EPISODE 19: "BAD BET ON A 459—SILENT"
*Written by Judith and Robert Guy Barrows*
*Directed by Seymour Robbie*
*Guest Starring: Bert Freed, Brian Avery, Nicolas Coster, Barry Ford, Jason Wingreen, Bud Perkins and Dick Dial*
A pair of corrupt police officers implicate the Green Hornet in a robbery, and he has to clear his name while bringing the cops to justice. When the Hornet is shot while trying to bring this happy result about, the world becomes much more complicated for the forces of good.

EPISODE 20: "ACE IN THE HOLE"
*Written by J.E. Selby and Stanley H. Silverman*
*Directed by William Baudine*
*Guest Starring: Richard Anderson, Richard X. Slattery, Bill Couch, Tony Epper, Perry Helton and Bill Hampton*
The Green Hornet and Kato rescue the kidnapped district attorney, while manipulating the kidnappers in such a way that they suspect each other of a double-cross.

*EPISODE 21: "TROUBLE FOR PRINCE CHARMING"*
*Written by Ken Pettus*
*Directed by William Baudine*
*Guest Starring: Edmund Hashim, Susan Flannery, Alberto Morin and James Lenphier*
The American fiance of a foreign prince is kidnapped as she's enroute to the airport to greet him. Those responsible demand that the foreign prince abdicate his throne if he ever wants to see her alive again. The prince feels that he has no choice, but the Green Hornet and Kato provide him with another option. In the end, the prince and his love are reunited and the kidnappers get their just desserts.

*EPISODE 22: "ALIAS THE SCARF"*
*Written by William L. Stuart*
*Directed by Allen Reisner*
*Guest Starring: John Carradine, Patricia*
A serial killer named the Scarf, who has not been seen or heard from in 20 years, comes out of "retirement" and renews his reign of terror. The reason? He feels that the Green Hornet and Kato are surpassing his notoriety. Of course, in the end, the Green Hornet and Kato still reign supreme.

*EPISODE 23: "HORNET, SAVE THYSELF"*
*Written by Don Tait*
*Directed by Seymour Robbie*
*Guest Starring: Michael Strong, Marvin Brody, Frank Marth, Ken Strange and Jack Perkins*
An enemy of Brit Reid's uses a radio-controlled gun to murder a man, then arranges the evidence to lead to Reid. The Green Hornet and Kato must clear his name before he is spends the rest of his life in a dank cell or is marched off to the executioner. Naturally justice prevails.

*EPISODE 24: "INVASION FROM OUTER SPACE", PART ONE*
*Written by Art Weingarten*
*Directed by Darrel Hallenbeck*
*Guest Starring: Larry D. Mann, Arthur Batanides, Christopher Dark, Linda Gaye Scott, Benny Dobbins, Joe di Reda, Brett King, Frank Babich, Lloyd Haynes, Troy Melton and Jerry Catron*

*EPISODE 25: "INVASION FROM OUTER SPACE", PART TWO*
*Written by Art Weingarten*
*Directed by Darrel Hallenbeck*
*Guest Starring: Brett King, Tyler McVey, Richard Poston and Bennie Dobbins*
A scientist and a group of people fake the landing of a UFO and the arrival of aliens. It's all a ruse to steal a hydrogen bomb in the midst of being transported by the military. The boys have to stop the hopeful nuclear thieves before nuclear holocaust rears its ugly head.

*EPISODE 26: "THE HORNET AND THE FIREFLY"*
*Written by William L. Stuart*
*Directed by Allen Reisner*
*Guest Starring: Gerald S. O'Loughlin, Russ Conway, Buff Brady and Gary Owens*
The Green Hornet and Kato pursue an arsonist. In the end, they disover he is really a fire inspector recently relieved from his position.

# Fists Of Fury

*BATMAN/GREEN HORNET CROSS OVER*
*TAKING PLACE DURING BATMAN'S SECOND SEASON*
*PART ONE: "A PIECE OF THE ACTION" /PART TWO: "BAT-*
*MAN'S SATISFACTION"*
*Written by Charles Hoffman*
*Directed by Oscar Rudolph*
*Starring: Adam West, Burt Ward, Alan Napier, Neil Hamilton, Stafford Repp and Madge Blake*
*Guest Starring: Van Williams, Bruce Lee, Diane McBain, Roger C. Carmel, Rico Cattani, Alex Rocco, Seymour Cassel, Harry Frazier, Dusty Cadis, Angelique Pettyjohn and Jan Watson*

The Green Hornet and Kato battle Batman and Robin to a stand-off [yeah, right, Robin manages to match the martial might of the greatest artist of them all!]. Ultimately Batman, Robin, the Green Hornet and Kato pool their energies to defeat stamp thief extraordinaire, Colonel Gumm.

# Bruce Lee

## CAST
Cheng: Bruce Lee
Mei: Maria Yi
Mi Han: Ying Chieh
Mi's Son: Tony Liu
Prostitute: Malalene
Chen: Paul Tien
Also featuring Miao Ke Hsui, Li Quin, Chin Shan and Li Hua Sze

## CREDITS
Screenplay and directed by Lo Wei
Produced by Raymond Chow
Art Direction: Chien Hsin
Fighting Instructor: Han Ying Chieh
Cinematography: Chen Ching Chu
Assistant Directors: Chin Yao Chang and Chen Cho
Assistant Producers: Liu Liang Hua and Lei Chen
A NATIONAL GENERAL PICTURES RELEASE
COLOR
MPAA RATING: R
RUNNING TIME: 103 MINUTES

# Fists Of Fury

## BEHIND THE SCENES

At the outset of 1970, Bruce Lee happened to go to a fortune teller, who informed him that the next year would be a highly successful one for him. Most people probably would have dismissed such a claim with a wave of a hand, but Bruce Lee had no doubt that she was right.

Bruce Lee, "the fastest fist in the east", as he is known throughout Hong Kong was born in San Francisco while his Chinese father toured the United States with a Chinese opera company.

"She predicted that 1971 will be my year," he told one journalist. "But I've already had this feeling that my time for success is here. I can just about taste it.

"After I left Hong Kong," he elaborated elsewhere, "the media there kept in contact with me through the telephone. Those guys used to call me early in the morning and even kept a conversation going on the air so the public was listening to me. Then one day the radio announcer asked me if I would do a movie there. When I replied that I would do it if the price was right, I began to get calls from producers in Hong Kong and Taiwan. Offers to do a movie varied from $2,000 to $10,000."

During this time he was inundated with offers for television series, but he was fearful of getting tied down to a long term contract. For example, Paramount wanted him to become a regular on **Longstreet**, but he only conceded to appearing on three more episodes. Several years later

Bruce Lee became involved in the development stage of a television martial arts series called *Kung Fu*, although he was never offered the role that eventually went to David Carradine. Additionally, Warner Brothers was interested in developing a television series for him, and the Run Run Shaw film company tried to interest him in a long-term contract. He turned them all down, instead waiting for the opportunity which he was convinced would come. Lee had to be true to himself, and the fate he felt lay before him.

He ultimately signed with Raymond Chow and Golden Harvest, who viewed Lee on a television special during which he demonstrated his martial arts skills.

Said Chow, "The demonstration Bruce gave on a TV show was very impressive. He kicked five one inch boards and broke four, and then kicked a dangling one inch board. That takes tremendous training and perfect timing. But what impressed me more is when I talked to him on a long distance call. He picked the most popular Hong Hong-based action picture of that time and asked a very blunt question. He asked me whether that was the best we could do. I had to say yes. Then he assured me with sincerity and confidence that he could do much better. How could I doubt this man?"

"After I signed with Raymond," Lee told *Black Belt* magazine, "I received a call from a producer in Taiwan. That guy told me to rip up the contract and he'd top Raymond's

---

**FISTS OF FURY BRINGS CHINESE KARATE/KUNG FU TO SCREEN**

Acting on the theme of "Blood and Revenge", *Fists of Fury* allows its star, American born Bruce Lee, to display a combination of self defense, Karate and the ancient Chinese art of illegal drug traffic, although set in modern day Hong Kong and Fu. Although keyed to a story of ing release allows Lee to show off his amazdogs and a man known as the "Big Boss" whose Kung Fu mastery is equal to that of the hero.

*Fists of Fury*, directed by Chinese film veteran Lo Wei, was the highest grossing motion picture to ever play the Orient. In addition to Bruce Lee, it features two Asian beauties, Hong Kong's Maria Yi and Taiwan's Malalene. (from the promotional material)

offer and even take care of any lawsuit for breaking the agreement."

Lee, a man of his word, never did break that contract. Instead he lived up to his commitment for two films. The first film was **The Big Boss** (retitled **Fists of Fury** in the United States). Although Lee found the conditions under which the films were made in Bangkok, Thailand terrible, the movie did allow him some personal gratification, particularly when compared to other films in the kung fu genre.

> **Fists of Fury** is the highest grossing film ever to play in Hong Kong. It has outgrossed The Sound of Music and Tora Tora Tora, the former record holders by more than $600,000 American dollars.

"They were awful," he stated. "For one thing, everybody fights all the time and what really bothered me was they all fought exactly the same way. Wow, nobody's really like that. When you get into a fight, everybody reacts differently and it is possible to act and fight at the same time.

"Most Chinese movies followed the Japanese," Lee added, "and there were too many weapons—especially swords. So we used a minimum of weapons and made it a better film. I mean people like films that are more than just one long, armed hassle. With any luck, I hope to make multilevel films here—the kind of movies where you can just watch the surface story, if you like, or can look deeper into it. Most of the Chinese films to date have been very superficial and one dimensional. I tried to change that in **The Big Boss**. The character I played was a very simple, straight-

forward guy. Like if you told this guy something, he'd believe you. Then, when he finally figures out how he's been had, he goes animal. This isn't a bad character, but I don't want to play him all the time. I'd prefer somebody with a little more depth."

**The Big Boss** was released in October of 1971, and went on to break a variety of foreign box office records, outgrossing *The Sound of Music* and becoming Hong Kong's number one money making film.

When this news reached Lee, his reaction, as so much of his life, was strong and colorful.

"We knew from the outset that the film was going to be a success," he said, "but I have to admit we weren't really expecting it to be *that* successful."

He hadn't seen anything yet!

> *Because most Chinese actors do not speak Mandarin, the official language of China, Fists of Fury was shot without sound. Then a team of skilled dubbers came in to make the soundtrack.*

## THE STORY

Cheng arrives in Bangkok to work at a local factory, as his uncle has arranged. He will be living with his cousins. In the course of the duo's conversation, the uncle tells Cheng to avoid fights and to remember his "promise". They approach a food cart to get something to eat and drink. While they're sitting, a group of punks start harassing the woman working the stand. Cheng is about to get involved, but his uncle holds him down, touches the locket hanging around his neck and says, "Remember your promise."

In the next moment, the punks steal a little boy's rice cakes and start slapping him around. Cheng's cousin Chen fights the punks in retribution, beating them all with some good moves and incredibly loud sound effects. Cheng meets the rest of his cousins and the woman Chow Mei, who obviously finds him attractive, which embarrasses Cheng.

We cut to the ice factory where Cheng is about to go to work. Uncle tells him to mind his own business and he'll be alright. While Cheng is being shown around, the factory Manager is involved in a drug transaction. Later, the Manager greets Cheng in a friendly manner.

That night, Chen tries to help a friend by getting her husband out of a gambling hall. He gives his buddy some cash and sends him home. Workers of the gambling hall don't take kindly to his interference and attack, but Chen beats them all. We can see that Cheng is dying to get involved, but the locket around his neck reminds him that he can't. It's a promise he made his mother before she died.

> *Lo Wei, the Chinese director of Fists of Fury, has directed more than 30 motion pictures in his native Hong Kong.*

The next day, Cheng goes to work and is verbally abused by the brusque Foreman, who tells him to get to work. Cheng loads a block of ice on the conveyer, but it slips and smashes apart, revealing packages of drugs inside. Only two people have seen. The driver of an awaiting truck punches Cheng in retribution for the broken ice and all the workers scare the driver off. At the end of the day, the Foremen tells the two men who saw the drugs that the Manager wants to see them right away.

The Manager tells them that now that they've seen the drugs, the Big Boss would like them to join the operation, and he offers them a thousand yen each. The men refuse, but promise they won't say anything. On the way home, they're murdered, their bodies then sliced by the factory's buzz-saw and the pieces encased in ice.

Next day, the workers are at the factory, wondering what happened to their cousins. Chen goes to the Manager, who says the two men had gone to see the Boss. Returning to the other men, Chen reveals his concern.

At his home, the Big Boss gives a kung fu demonstration to his son and his friends. Later, he meets with Chen and one other worker who express their dismay at the disappearance. The Boss says he gave the men a bonus for doing such a good job and they left. That's the last he's heard of them. When they press him further, he states that they had better stop meddling or they'll be sorry. Angry, the two men depart, but as they make their way across the property, they're attacked by a group of men. Chen and the other man are killed.

That night, everyone is worried sick, as now there are four men missing. Next day, everyone begins to investigate. The Manager tells them that the Boss is investigating the disappearances. The workers think that something sinister has happened. The bell to start work rings, but

---

**BRUCE LEE—ASIA'S FIRST SUPERSTAR THE MAN WITH THE "FISTS OF FURY"**

Unarmed, the quietly smiling Chinese moves steadily into the ring of knife brandishing villains. For a long moment, the audience sucks in its breath. Then, in a split second, he leaps into the air, his arms and legs whirring in a flurry of punches and kicks that unerringly find their mark. Before one can say "Lee Hsian Lung", the hero of Chinese cinema has downed a dozen villains twice his size and cheers echo throughout a packed movie house. Bruce Lee, as he is known through China, is never in real danger in **Fists of Fury**, the first "karate-kung fu" movie that has set all the attendance records in the Far East. For his millions of fans around the world, Lee's fighting prowess is what it is all about. Most of all it has transformed the 32 year old American actor into Asia's first superstar—the epitome of high living, the heart-throb of thousands of adoring girls and the idol of young overseas Chinese from New York to Taipe.

Lee relies heavily for his success on a formula of rippling muscles and a sort of "yellow power". His name means "Little Dragon" and he retains a strong American accent and admits that his tastes were acquired in the United States. The son of a popular opera star, he was born in San Francisco. Lee is 5 foot 7 inches tall and was running a school in Hong Kong where he taught his personal adaptation of Chinese jeet kune do boxing when Hong Kong movie magnate Raymond Chow offered him a role in **Fists of Fury**, which broke all Hong Kong box office records. Bruce Lee came very close to being the ultimate mid-pacific man, what with all the good things happening to him on both sides of the ocean. His background emanates from both the Far East and the Far West; he is married to an American girl and they have two international children. Bruce Lee understands the publics of both countries. "Action is what the people want right now and in **Fists of Fury** it's what they are getting." (from the promotional material)

they refuse to move. The Foreman and his men start beating the workers. Cheng wants to step in, but his enigmatic promise prevents him from doing so. Reinforcements from the Boss arrive and they start to savagely beat the workers. One of them attacks Cheng, ripping the locket from his neck and smashing it. This seems to be the final motivation, as Cheng lets out a cry of fury and leaps into the brawl, taking out men left and right. He turns to them and states that the workers can't be pushed around, and then offers to take them all on. They accept, and in a fluid poetry of motion, he knocks some out, sending the others in retreat. The cousins applaud what he's done. Then the manager says he wants to see Cheng in his office. While they're waiting to see what's going on, a notice is posted stating that Cheng is the new Foreman, and they all rejoice upon his promotion. Chew Mei takes everyone to task as they've forgotten the missing men.

Next day, Cheng speaks to the Manager and is told that the Boss has gone to the police. Cheng feels that if the men don't show up by nightfall, they should go to the authorities themselves. A meeting is arranged between Cheng, the Manager and the Boss, but the Boss doesn't doesn't show up. The Manager states that he had an important business meeting. He adds that the next morning the Boss will be meeting with the chief of police to find out what's going on, and that by Friday the men will be back on the job. Cheng and the manager have dinner, and prostitutes arrive. Everyone works on getting Cheng drunk, and they're quite successful in this endeavor.

> Linda Lee, the American born wife of Hong Kong superstar Bruce Lee, first met him while they were both students at the University of Seattle.

Meanwhile, the others are concerned that Cheng hasn't come home, fearing that he is now among the missing. Back at the Manager's, Cheng is in bed with one of the

women, but he has passed out. He awakens the next morning, completely unaware of what had happened the night before. He leaves, but Chow Mei catches him and realizes what he's been doing. He comes back to the factory and everyone is angry that he didn't go to the police like he said he would. He goes to the Manager and says that he would like to see the Boss, who, on the phone, agrees to a meeting.

After work, Cheng goes to the designated meeting place. As he enters the property, he is attacked by three guard dogs, but is able to keep leaping out of their way until the Boss stops them. When Cheng is invited in, the Boss starts smoking opium and apologizes for the lack of information concerning his cousins. Everything goes smoothly, until a servant spills tea and gets struck with a dart—courtesy of the Boss—as her punishment. Cheng has an expression which says he has put this on a mental checklist. The Boss will continue turning the town upside down to find the men. Once Cheng has departed, Boss states that the man is suspicious and must be watched very carefully.

> *Bruce Lee, the star of Fists of Fury, taught self defense to actor Lee Marvin for the latter's role in The Professionals.*

Rejected by his cousins who feel he's betrayed them, Cheng goes back to the prostitute he had been with the night before and expresses his worry over the missing men. She tells him to be careful, explaining that these people are dangerous. They *don't* make their money from ice, but rather from the drugs placed within. She adds that she used to work for the Boss and shows Cheng the scars from where she was struck with his darts. Without a word, Cheng leaves. An instant later, the Boss' son enters her room and stabs her to death.

Meanwhile, Chow Mei is hanging clothes when she is kidnapped by the Boss' people, as his son has been promised her as a plaything. The men then proceed into the house, their intentions quite clear.

Cheng breaks into the warehouse and chips away at some blocks of ice, finding the drugs hidden within. Upon further investigation, he discovers his cousins' bodies as well. Then the lights go up and he is surrounded by the Boss' people. All hell breaks loose as Lee swings into action with smashing fists and flashing feet. Everything is a blur of motion. Surprisingly, however, he does so via knives and a saw as well as his body. Such weapons would be given up in future films.

The fight leads outside, where Cheng continues winning, but the Boss' son slashes him with a knife. Cheng tastes the blood and grows even more furious. Their battle ends with Cheng ripping out the man's intestines.

> Bruce Lee, who created a box office bonanza in Hong Kong with his first film, Fists of Fury, is no stranger to American audiences. Lee played Kato in The Green Hornet TV series, and was seen opposite James Garner in the film Marlowe.

Repulsed by his own violence, he goes home. Lee performs beautifully in the role, conveying his emotions, and looking like a little boy who has done something wrong and is afraid of the consequences. Once inside the house, he's horrified to find that all of his cousins have been slaughtered and Chow Mei is nowhere to be found. He breaks down and starts to cry, cradling a cousin's head in his lap.

Next morning, Cheng sits before a brook, his mind racing with thoughts we hear via a voiceover. He feels that everything he has dreamed of has been destroyed. The Boss and his people must pay for what they've done, even at the cost of his own life.

Cheng arrives at the Boss' home and leaps over the fence. Six men confront him with knives. Using hands, feet and his own knives, he quickly eliminates these would be kill-

ers and approaches the Boss. When they face each other, the screen erupts into battle. This sequence offers spectacular shots of Lee kicking and punching at the camera, which are quite effective.

While this battle takes place, the Boss' servant frees Chow Mei. Outside, the Boss, who is now armed with a pair of knives, manages to slash Cheng's face, leg and chest. The knives are thrown, but Cheng deflects them with his feet and sends the blades deep into the Boss' chest. He collapses, dead. This doesn't stop Cheng, who begins pummeling the man's face with his fists.

The police arrive and surround Cheng. Chow Mei tries to embrace him as he is led to the waiting squad car.

And so ends Bruce Lee's first film, an effective piece of martial arts camerawork and storytelling.

*One of the most expensive props in Bruce Lee's film Fists of Fury is gallons of fake blood used for the many kung fu-karate battles.*

While the story is pretty much standard fare, and fights sometimes break out for no reason whatsoever (which is the nature of the beast, one must assume), Lee makes it fully believable, with sincere emotions showcased by Cheng's reactions to external torments. The fight scenes, even in this early film, were superior to most of what had come before Lee or that would come after his departure form moviemaking. The only disquieting aspect, as noted above, is that Lee relies so heavily on weapons, in this case, knives. Eventually he would move on to stick fighting and the nunchuka.

Considering that this was the first serious attempt by Lee to create a martial arts epic, the result is not at all disappointing.

## **PRODUCTION NOTES**

(from the kit released with the movie)

At the outset of the 1960s, film makers and film goers alike were turned on to the motorcycle pictures that emanated from Hollywood. These had superseded the beach party films and served as the antecedents for the "horror" film, the "spaghetti western" phenomenon and ultimately the black exploitation films. Now, a new "genre" is emerging. This time Hollywood has been left out and from Hong Kong and Taiwan comes a series of Oriental films with "blood and revenge" as their themes. American born Bruce Lee has become an Asian superstar and his first film, **Fists of Fury**, has been acquired by National General Pictures for distribution in America.

Aside from the cost of film stock itself, the single greatest outlay in the Chinese "karate-Kung Fu" movies goes for synthetic blood. Between 3%-5% of the budget regularly buys innumerable half gallon plastic bottles of red sticky liquid. "At the close of the day's shooting," a scripwriter remarked, "a typical set looks like a front line dressing station after a major battle. We Chinese are a violent people—and that's what audiences want." The appeal of blood is not limited to Chinese patrons in Taiwan, Hong Kong and Southeast Asia. The themes of these films have attracted wide audiences in South America, Africa and the Middle East.

Revenge is a basic Chinese passion dating back to Confucian times. He himself warned against the passion 2,500 years ago. The vendetta was a fixture of Chinese society long before Sicilians and hillbillies adopted the blood feud. **Fists of Fury** places the emphasis on unarmed fighting (kung fu) rather than the old fashioned sword fighting. The "spaghetti westerns" helped to launch Clint Eastwood as an international star and now these "karate-kung fu" films will do the same for Bruce Lee. Lee is the hottest property in the Chinese movie industry, its first superstar. He has been dubbed "the fastest fist in the east". Small boys—and some very big boys—regularly challenge him to fight when they spy him on the streets. Sometimes he accepts, for he is full of suppressed violence engendered by a singularly unhappy childhood. Bruce Lee was born in San Francisco while his Chinese opera star father was touring the States. He grew up in Hong Kong where he was regularly expelled from schools till, when he was 18, his father sent him back to the States "where all the kids are impossible." He played a few small parts in television dramas and was finally discovered on a quick trip back to Hong Kong. His first film, **Fists of Fury**, broke all attendance records.

Because more Chinese actors do not speak fluent Mandarin, the official language of China, all of the productions are shot without sound. Then a team of skilled dubbers come in to make the sound track.

## PROMOTIONS

- **KARATE KRAZE:** Karate schools have loomed all over the country. Arrange tie-ins with local schools on a contest basis and center an opening day activity around an in-theatre lobby demonstration of this lethal art of Chinese self defense.
- **FASHIONS:** The recent visit of President Nixon to Peking stirred a new interest in things oriental, especially clothing. Use **Fists of Fury** stills in windows of stores featuring the Chinese designed garments.
- **SPECIAL EVENTS:** Let your most prominent local DJ sponsor a midnight showing of the film for his listeners. Make sure the event is supported by plenty of on-station radio spots and newspaper ads for which they pick up the cost.
- **RESTAURANT TIE-IN:** Let's not forget the popular Chinese restaurant as an excellent site for displays and as a prize in a contest.
- **CONTESTS:** The art of Karate and Kung Fu are specially skilled talents. Sponsor a local contest centered around physical competitions from Boxing to Table Tennis.
- **ADVANCE WORD:** Be sure to spread the word about the phenomenal Karate Kung Fu through advanced previews of the movie and especially through early showings of the exciting trailer. (from the promotional booklet)

When the Shanghai movie community migrated en masse in 1949 just before the Communist takeover, only a few films were made in Hong Kong and all of them were made in the Catonese dialect. The new arrivals experienced hard times and they were able to make the only kind of films they knew: dramas of social protest or nationalistic exhortation. This new founded prosperity is a welcome change for the Hong Kong movie community.

One of the most famous of all Chinese directors and the director of **Fists of Fury** is Lo Wei. In more than 35 years in the business, Lo Wei has supplied his deft directorial touch to 75 feature films. In addition to directing **Fists of Fury**, he also wrote the action packed script and he is of the opinion that these "karate-kung fu" films are here to stay. "People want to see action," he says. "In a fast moving world people are interested in action. They do not like sitting through dull non-action films. It is too slow." Almost half of Lo Wei's films have been action films so it was not too surprising that he was chosen to direct **Fists of Fury**. When questioned on the violence in these films, Lo Wei said, "I believe that there has to be some violence in a film of this type, but the way it is treated in **Fists of Fury** (rather tongue in cheek) is the proper way of doing it. It has been grossly exaggerated and somehow the audience rather laughs at it and realizes the futility of violence. I'm proud of **Fists of Fury** and am pleased that western audiences will get a chance to see our work."

**CAST**
Chen Chen: Bruce Lee
Yuan Li-erh: Miao Ker Hsui
Fan Chun-Hsia: James Tien
Russian Boxer: Robert Baker

**CREDITS**
Producer: Raymond Chow
Director: Lo Wei
Cinematographer: Chen Ching-Chu
Assistant Producer: Liu Liang Hua
Production Designer: Lo Wei
Assistant Director: Chin Yao-Ching
Screenplay: Lo Wei
Editor: Chang Ching-Chu
Music Composed By Ku Chi-Hui
Fighting Instructor: Hen Ying Chieh
A National General Pictures Corp. Release
Color
MPAA Rating: R
Running Time: 107 Minutes

## BEHIND THE SCENES

Distribution of film across oceans was slow process in the early 1970s. It took time for the retitled **Fists of Fury** to arrive in American theaters from Asia. By the time the film reached American movie screens, the kung fu craze had already begun to hit, thanks in large part to Warner Brothers' pick-up of *Five Fingers of Death*. That film encapsulated what the genre would fundamentally represent: lots of gratuitous violence and gore, improbable leaps, mid-air battles, fights resembling complicated ballets and unbelievable sound effects. Nonetheless, films of the genre brought a tremendous sense of escapism to American audiences; one that touched a chord with theater-goers, paving the way for innumerable imports. The violence of the screen provided a safe catharsis to relieve the frustrations and tensions of everyday living.

Bruce Lee's **Fists of Fury**, conversely, gave the first early indications of what a genre *could* be. While lacking some of the elements that Lee would later present in **Enter the Dragon** and certain moments of **Game of Death**, it offered a touch more realism and a protagonist who didn't need cinematic special effects to make him look good on screen.

**The Chinese Connection (Fists of Fury** in the Orient—is this getting confusing yet?) was another tremendous hit, breaking the box office records set by its predecessor and giving every indication that Bruce Lee was going in directions no other Asian star had gone before. He was a worldwide sensation, plain and simple, and his popularity seemed to be boundless.

Dealing with this success was not always easy, as Lee detailed to *Fighting Stars* magazine. "I had people stop by my door and just pass me a check for $200,000," Lee said. "When I asked them what it was for, they replied, 'Don't worry, it's just a gift for you.' I mean, I didn't even know these people. When people pass big money like that, you don't know what to think. I destroyed all the checks, but it was difficult to do, because I didn't know what they were for. Sure, money is important in providing for my family, but it isn't everything...I didn't know who to trust and I even grew suspicious of my old pals. I was in a period when I didn't know who was trying to take advantage of me."

One thing Lee was fully aware of was what he hoped to receive from his film career, as emphasized from these quotes culled from various sources which were printed in Ohara Publications' *The Bruce Lee Story*:

"Ever since I was a kid, the word quality has meant a great deal to me. The greatest satisfaction is to hear another unbiased human being whose heart has been touched and honestly says, 'Hey, here is someone real!' I'd like that! In my life, what can you ask for but to be real, to fulfill one's mission and above all, actualize one's potential instead of dissipating one's image, which is not real and expending one's vital energy. We have great work ahead of us and it needs devotion and much, much energy. To grow, to discover, we need involvement, which is something I experience every day, sometimes good, sometimes frustrating. No matter what, you let your inner light guide you out of darkness.

"I'm dissatisfied with the expression of the cinematic art here in Hong Kong. It's time somebody did something about the films here. There are simply not enough soulful characters here who are committed, dedicated and are at the same time professionals. I believe I have a role. The audience needs to be educated and the one to educate them has to be somebody who is responsible. We are dealing with the masses and we have to educate them step by step. We can't do it overnight. That's what I'm doing right now. Whether I succeed or not remains to be seen. But I just don't *feel* committed, I *am* committed.

"I didn't create this monster—all this gore in the Mandarin films. It was there before I came. At least I don't spread violence. I don't call the fighting in my films violence. I call it action. An action film borders somewhere between reality and fantasy. If it were completely realistic, you would call me a bloody, violent man. I would simply destroy my opponent by tearing him apart or ripping his guts out. I wouldn't do it so artistically. I have this intensity in me that the audience believes in what I do because I do believe in what I do. But I act in such a way as to border my action somewhere between reality and fantasy.

"I can't even express myself fully on film here, or the audience wouldn't understand what I am talking about half the time. That's why I can't stay in Southeast Asia all the time. I am improving and making new discoveries every day. If you don't, you are already crystallized and that's it. I'll be doing different types of films in the future, some serious, some philosophical and some pure entertainment. But I will never prostitute myself in any way."

**BRUCE LEE KARATE KUNG-FU ADVENTURE TO OPEN**

The Chinese Connection tells the story of the conflict between two schools of Chinese and Japanese martial training. American-born Bruce Lee displays a combination of karate and the ancient Chinese art of self defense, Kung-Fu, in the adventure set in modern-day Hong Kong (sic). The Chinese Connection, directed by Chinese film veteran Lo Wei (Fists of Fury), was one of the most successful motion pictures to ever play in the Orient. The film features Miao Ker Hsiu, Robert Baker and James Tien. National General Pictures is releasing. (from the promotional material)

As if to make good on his word, Bruce Lee set upon his next film project: **Way of the Dragon**, retitled **Return of the Dragon** for American release and unveiled *after* his death and the release of **Enter the Dragon**. This time Lee not only starred in and choreographed the fight sequences, but he wrote and directed as well.

## THE STORY

The time and place: 1908, Shanghai. A famous Chinese martial artist has died and we open on his funeral. Chen Chen (Bruce Lee) arrives and we can see the emotional pain he's undergoing as he screams out in disbelief. From the outset, Lee is adding something new and different to the character he played in **Fists of Fury**. It's a bit surprising to watch him collapse at the teacher's grave, crying as he tries to dig up the man. The emotional intensity we are watching is not something we would expect.

Two days pass and we learn that Chen has been meditating before a photo of Teacher and has not eaten anything during that time. He finally talks to his fellow students, demanding to know what Teacher had died of and is told pneumonia. Further conversation ensues, however, and reveals that everyone has their suspicions as to the actual cause of Teacher's death. They all plan to investigate the many possibilities. A subsequent eulogy states that the philosophy behind Teacher's lessons was to develop their minds and characters, and that they will all have to honor his memory.

A moment later, Woo, representing a rival Japanese school, arrives and addresses the students, issuing a warning: they had better disband if they know what's good for them. He claims they will never be as good as the Japanese martial artists. Woo drops a challenge, hoping to humiliate their champion into stepping forward. Chen steps forward, but is held back. The Chinese leader says that their style of study is for purposes of peace and *defense* only. The barrage of insults continues, but Chen is still held back. Frustrated, Woo and his people leave.

The next day, Chen arrives at the Japanese school and delivers his own challenge to any Japanese in the room. One man, rather confident in his abilities, steps forward, but is quickly eliminated. A second man follows suit, then a third, until all the students surround Chen. At this point in the film, director Lo Wei uses an overhead shot that gives us a full view of movement as all involved move in perfect synchronization. Strangely enough, it reminds the viewer of the old MGM musicals which were choreographed to such perfection. The dance of death simulates a more tra

ditional ballet, which, of course, often included action and death scenes as well.

Chen removes his shirt in preparation and then enters his fighting stance. Everyone moves in for the kill, but are beaten back, only to come back for more. Chen grabs a nunchuka and utilizes it to great effect. The director executes an effective close-up of Lee's eyes at this point, as Lee's character carefully watches his opponents. Then Chen drops to the floor and starts smashing the legs of the students, who all collapse.

One man approaches. Chen throws the nunchuka away, then confidently folds his arms across his chest. The man holds maintains even ground in the fight for a while, but is eventually defeated. Chen puts on his shirt, picks up his nunchuka and leaves, the Japanese cowering in fear. Woo arrives outside just as Chen knocks out two more students, but he remains unseen.

Suzuki, the Japanese leader, is quite displeased with the report of what happened when Chen appeared, and tells Woo that they should tear apart the Chinese school. He orders them not to return if they fail.

Chen arrives in a park area, but is denied admission as the guard points to a sign which reads, "No Chinese or Dogs Allowed". Then some Japanese approach, with one stating that if he wants to get in, all Chen has to do is act like a dog and the man is sure he'll be able to get him through. Chen responds by knocking the man out and eliminating the other Japanese. Then he destroys the sign in a symbolic gesture.

Students of the Chinese school are training. The Japanese arrive and an all-out brawl ensues, with much of the school and the memorial to Teacher being destroyed in the ensuing violence. The damage done, Woo stops the fight and declares they have three days to hand Chen over to them or their school *will* be closed. Once they are gone, the Chinese wonder if Chen is indeed the one who started this whole thing. As if in answer, Chen arrives and admits he had gone to the Japanese. One of the students replies, "You act the hero, and here's what happens to us." They tell Chen to leave Shanghai, but he is not able to. It's the only solution that will save both him and their school, they insist, and Chen recognizes this to be fact.

That night, Chen is in the midst of meditating when he hears strange noises. He catches sight of two men removing poisoned biscuits before the students can learn that this is what caused Teacher's death. Chen confronts them with the fact that they were only pretending to be Chinese students, and then repeats his now famous **Fists of Fury** rip out the intestines trick on one of them. The second man tries to kill Chen with an axe, but fails miserably. Chen demands to know why they killed Teacher. Instead of learning the answer, Chen beats the man to death while trying to find out. At this point in the film, Lee does an excellent job of demonstrating the volatile nature of Chen's personality, providing an interesting contrast to the more thoughtful and philosophical Cheng in **Fists of Fury**.

A note is left for the Chinese students. The note explains the truth of the poisoned biscuits and that Chen is seeking revenge for the death of their beloved mentor. Meanwhile,

the bodies of the two men are hung from a lamp post. The police arrive and cut them down. The Chinese feel they will be blamed for the murders. They realize that Chen is the one responsible and that they've got to find him.

That night, Chen is found by a woman from the school who tries to convince him to come back. He won't, merely saying that he is *not* hiding, but rather has made "plans". He believes that Woo knows about Teacher's death.

The next morning, Woo tells Suzuki about what happened to the two men secretly placed in the Chinese school. Suzuki is aware of what has transpired between Chen and the spies. One of the men wants revenge, but Woo insists they should give the school an ultimatum: hand over Chen or the police will close the school. "Chen is too gallant for that," he smiles, "so he'll turn himself over." Suzuki agrees to their plan.

The police are at the Chinese school, demanding to know who hung the two men and where Chen is. They swear they don't know. The police give them two days to hand him over, or else the school will be shut down.

Elsewhere, Suzuki is having dinner with Woo and a Russian boxer, watching a Japanese stripper. The Russian says that now that he's been in Shanghai, he's Suzuki's "man", which pleases him to no end. A very drunk Woo excuses himself and catches a ride on a rickshaw, which unbeknownst to him is being pulled by Chen, who turns down a alley with no other exit. They come to a stop and Woo is horrified to find Chen standing before him, demanding an explanation for what has transpired. Woo tearfully admits that Suzuki ordered the death of Teacher. Then he starts pleading for his life. Chen spares him, and when he turns to leave, Woo attacks. In the fight, Chen kills Woo. His body is found hanging the next morning.

## Fists Of Fury

Suzuki puts pressure on the police. Either something must be done, or his school will take the matter into their own deadly hands. The police return to the school and are once again told that the students don't know where Chen is. One more day is given before the school will be closed. All of the students will go to prison if Chen doesn't show up.

The woman shown earlier tells the Chinese leader that she knows where Chen stays at night. While this conversation is going on, Chen keeps aware of events by travelling under disguise, first as an elderly newspaper vendor and then as a telephone repairman. Under the latter guise, Chen uses to infiltrates Suzuki's school. There he sees the Russian in training, demonstrating his prowess by pushing nails through wood with his bare hands and bending metal pipes. Chen is amused by this silly, useless exercise. Still in disguise, Chen is led into Suzuki's office to repair the phone. Suzuki mentions (and this is pretty stupid on his part) that he would love to kill Chen, and his subordinate says they should concentrate on the school instead. Chen leaves and once he does, the subordinate says they should kill the Chinese students, thus removing any possible evidence against them of murder. Suzuki agrees, emphasizing that no one can be left alive. Every student must be painfully and ruthlessly killed.

That night, a group of the Chinese students go to Chen's hiding place, while Chen goes to Suzuki's school, easily wiping out a group of students with his hands and feet. Then he comes up against a Japanese armed with a Samurai sword, but is able to avoid the blade and wins by kicking the sword into the air, grabbing his opponent and pulling him forward so that the descending blade cuts right through him. It's a sensational moment in the history of martial arts film!

Chen continues on until confronted by still more students. Suzuki and the Russian watch the entire fight. Then the Russian approaches Chen. They start to fight and Chen immediately seems to be in trouble, but he begins smiling as his kicks and punches make *serious* contact with the Russian. The fight culminates when he smashes the Russian's throat, crushing his windpipe. Next Chen fights Suzuki, who is armed with a sword. Chen whips out his nunchuka and uses it to deflect the blade, ultimately disarming the man. Then they turn to hand-to-hand combat. Both Suzuki and Chen leap into the air, as Chen connects his swinging foot with the other man's throat, sending his corpse crashing through a wall.

The Chinese students return home to find those who had remained behind, now dead or dying. At that moment, the leader states that Chen was right and they should have stood up to Suzuki before this. The police and Japanese

---

## BRUCE LEE, AN ASIAN-AMERICAN SUPERSTAR DISCUSSES KARATE/KUNG-FU

Bruce Lee, an American born Chinese, who found world-wide fame as the star of **Fists of Fury** and now in **The Chinese Connection**...first learned about Kung-Fu as a teenager. His father taught him the rudimentary principles and as Lee explains, "I was hooked on it from there on. My father sent me to study with Yip Man, a famous Hong Kong teacher of the Wing-chuen Kune style of Kung-Fu, which I later modified; the technique I use in my films is one that I call Jeet Kune Do. Basically, it uses more foot work than the more elementary style."

Lee, who earned a Masters Degree in Philosophy from the University of Washington, wrote his thesis on Kung-Fu. It was later expanded into a book which was published in 1963 by the Oriental Book Sales of Oakland, California and called Chinese Kung-Fu, the Philosophical Art of Self Defense.

"It was difficult for me to start my career in America," Lee says, "since roles for Chinese were rare and those that were available always given to Japanese; so immediately after my graduation I opened the Bruce Lee-Jung Fan Kung-Fu Institute in Seattle. This school taught the Jeet Kune Do style of Kung-Fu. This style is more dramatic and spectacular and stresses brevity. The great leaps are all part of the Jeet Kune Do style."

In the early 1960's, the word karate was already familiar to the American public, but the groin kicks and eye gouges that are used weren't ready to be accepted. However, the film companies were eager to use this flashy martial art and found that by assigning karate and Kung-Fu to the bad guys, the public would accept it. For quite a few years, the karate fighters in American motion pictures were always the bad guys. The turnabout came in 1964 when the James Bond movies used a superficial form of karate as a self defense to defeat the enemies of justice. In 1967 the final breakthrough came with the **Green Hornet** TV series in which Bruce Lee played Kato and became the first practitioner of Kung-Fu to demonstrate incredible combat techniques that had never been seen before. This was the first accurate depiction of the Oriental Martial Arts shown to a wide general public.

Bruce Lee, the first American born Asian superstar, has never stopped working on his technique. **The Chinese Connection** shows even more of this incredible self defense mechanism. National General Pictures is releasing as they did the earlier **Fists of Fury**. (from the promotional material)

consul arrive and start searching for Chen. They are shocked at the carnage laying all about.

Chen climbs through a window of a room on the second floor and finds even more bodies of the dead. Fury is born in him anew. Overhearing his "brothers" being arrested, a tearful Chen comes down the stairs. He goes to the police chief and wants to know if the police will leave the Chinese school alone if he turns himself in. The chief solemnly gives his word that the school will be left in peace.

Chen steps outside and sees an army of men with weapons aimed at him. A rebel with a cause, he runs and leaps at them. Freeze-frame of Chen in mid-air, the sound of gunshots filling the soundtrack.

Despite the fact that the mainstream movie audience might dismiss **The Chinese Connection** as a "mass market" king fu film, it really is far more than that. The plot focuses on racial prejudice and it's terrible costs. Bruce Lee's Chen is the most outraged victim. Chinese and Japanese. Black and white. American and Indian. It's all pretty interchangeable, as the sad result remains the same, the moral degrading of both races. This film is also considerably different from **Fists of Fury** in terms of the main character and the tools he uses to achieve his goals. In the last film, Lee's Cheng was more introspective and philosophical, pondering the ramifications of his every move in an attempt to fulfill a promise to his dying mother. It was only after being pushed to his limits that he fought back.

This time the characterization of the main protagonist, Chen, in **The Chinese Connection** is quite different. While just as committed to his beliefs as Cheng had been, Chen needs only a nudge to begin violently fighting back. He will *not* be pushed. The one drawback to this approach is that it's a little more difficult to identify with the hero as

quickly as we need to, but overall it does work. A positive change in this film is that Lee no longer uses knives, choosing instead to let his body be a lethal weapon, aided only by the nunchuka.

There is an interesting aspect to both **Fists of Fury** and **The Chinese Connection** that makes it different from American-made action films. Normally in the American cinema, an action hero is pushed until he has to fight back,

and then the attitude is to let the chips fall where they may. Never do they have to face charges for the lives they have taken, or the damage they've caused. Can you imagine James Bond or Dirty Harry going to jail? In Chinese films, conversely, the hero most definitely pays a price, despite the fact that his actions are justified. In **Fists of Fury** Cheng successfully avenges the death of his family, but at the conclusion he is arrested for murder. In **The Chinese Connection**, Chen battles the racial intolerance of others while destroying the killer of his teacher and fellow students, but only at the cost of his own life.

Overall **The Chinese Connection** works, but the viewer can see that Bruce Lee needed to move in other directions, if only to spare himself from the oblivion that innumerable kung fu stars found themselves cast off to. If Lee hoped to succeed he would have to transcend the genre.

## PRODUCTION NOTES

(from the kit released with the movie)

**The Chinese Connection** was one of the most popular and successful motion pictures ever to play in Hong Kong. In dollars and cents, it grossed more than **Fists of Fury**, the first of the Kung-Fu pictures to be shown to western audiences. Bruce Lee, who starred in both, has become the first Asian superstar and it is as impossible for him to walk down the streets in China as it was for the Beatles to stroll down Carnaby Street in London during their heyday. It is Lee more than anyone else who has made Kung-Fu so popular. In Los Angeles, sales of Kung-Fu books have risen more than 50% since last January and businessmen are doing a brisk business in the sale of Kung-Fu uniforms. Unlike the hard, powerful style of karate, Kung-Fu involves softer, more fluid movements, all of which have philosophical meanings. It is a way of life and it is closely related to acupuncture. The same body points you use to heal a patient are the ones you use to hurt an opponent.

Aside from the cost of the film itself the single greatest outlay in **The Chinese Connection** is for synthetic blood. Almost 4% of the total budget goes to buy this red sticky liquid. Now, since some of these films have been seen in the United States, it is easier to understand their vast popularity. The themes of these films have attracted wide audiences in South America, Africa and the Middle East. It goes without saying that they are the most popular mass form of entertainment in Hong Kong and Taiwan.

Revenge is a basic Chinese passion and this is the basic ingredient in **The Chinese Connection**. Confucius himself warned against this passion more than 2,500 years ago. The vendetta has always been a form and fixture of Chinese society long before the Sicilians and hillbillies adopted the blood feud.

## CAST
Tang: Bruce Lee
Chen: Nora Miao
Colt: Chuck Norris
Bob: Robert Wall
Master of Hapkido: Wong In Sik

## CREDITS
Producer: Raymond Chow
Director: Bruce Lee
Screenplay: Bruce Lee
A Golden Harvest Production Released by Bryanston Pictures
MPAA Rating: R
Running Time: 91 Minutes

## BEHIND THE SCENES

Following the record breaking success of **The Chinese Connection** in the Orient, Bruce Lee could pretty much write his own ticket. The dual success of that film and **Fists of Fury** in the States brought Hollywood beating down his door. His two-picture contract with Raymond Chow had been fulfilled and he was now free to follow whatever path he chose.

For a time Lee seriously considered undertaking a collaboration with Chow on **The Yellow Faced Tiger**, but creative differences with proposed director Lo Wei ended in his leaving the project. Instead, Lee took destiny into his own hands launching his own production company—Concord Pictures. He took full creative control over **Way [Return] of the Dragon**. Produced in association with Raymond Chow, the film was eventually released in the U.S. *after* Lee's death and after **Enter the Dragon** appeared in theaters. In fact the new film was sold as a sequel.

The pressures of his newfound independence, and the needs of running his own business, often became trying for Lee. He was not fully prepared for the change from hired hand, no matter how valuable, to being his own boss and meeting the responsibilities of running his own company. Before this he was unaware of just how much others had shielded him from. But, as his personal system of beliefs demanded, he would try to learn to deal with the newfound responsibilities.

"To many," he told *Black Belt* magazine, "the word 'success' seems to be a paradise, but now that I'm in the midst of it all, it is nothing but circumstances that seem to complicate my innate feelings towards simplicity and privacy. Yet, like it or not, circumstances are thrust upon me and, being a fighter at heart, I sort of fight in the beginning, but soon realize what I need is not inner resistance and needless conflict in the form of dissipation; rather, by joining forces to readjust and make the best of it.

"I can't go wrong, because what I've always liked in myself is this 'stickability' toward quality and the sincere desire to do it right. In a way, I am glad that this prosperous happening is occurring to me when I am maturing to a state of readiness and definitely will not blow it because of 'self-glorification' as being 'blocked by illusion.' I am prepared."

It was this confidence that he brought to **Way of the Dragon** and it ultimately paid off handsomely, surpassing the record established in the Orient with **The Chinese Connection**.

"In **Way of the Dragon** I wrote the script, had the starring role, directed it and produced it," Lee explained. "I worked almost around the clock every day and lost several pounds. I did it because it was fun. It was something I hadn't done before, but always had an interest in. I got hold of a dozen books on film production and direction and really dug into them."

The film, discussed in the next section, showed definite signs of creative growth on Lee's part. The capable script was fully realized under his direction and his skills as an actor/martial artist seemed to continually progress. Another important aspect of the film, and one that separated it

---

**FISTS OF FURY BRINGS CHINESE KARATE/KUNG FU TO SCREEN**

Acting on the theme of "Blood and Revenge", **Fists of Fury** allows its star, American-born Bruce Lee, to display a combination of Karate and the ancient Chinese art of self-defense, Kung Fu. Although set in modern day Hong Kong and keyed to a story of illegal drug traffic, the National General Pictures release allows Lee to show off his amazing use of fists, feet and leaping against overwhelming odds of men, vicious attack dogs and a man known as the "Big Boss" whose Kung Fu mastery is equal to that of the hero.

**Fists of Fury**, directed by Chinese film veteran Lo Wei, was the highest grossing motion picture to ever play the Orient. In addition to Bruce Lee, it features two Asian beauties, Hong Kong's Maria Yi and Taiwan's Malalene. (from promotional material)

from other entries in the genre, was a certain sense of Americanization. **Way of the Dragon** was the first film from the Orient that utilized locales outside the country, in this case Rome, culminating in a final battle taking place in the remains of the ancient Roman Colosseum. In addition, Lee cast Italian actors as the villains and American karate champions Bob Wall and Chuck Norris as their henchmen. This made the film more commercial to Asian audiences, as noted by Linda Lee and Tom Bleecker in *The Bruce Lee Story*.

"The truly commercial aspect," they wrote, "was that the audience to which he was trying to appeal was Chinese—and the Chinese like to see their Chinese heroes conquering people of a different race. If that sounds like racial prejudice, perhaps it is understandable in view of the history of the Chinese people. But just as important to Bruce was the fact that he would be fighting professional karate men rather than actors or dancers, which he believed would give his film greater realism and authenticity."

Obviously he was right, because even America ultimately accepted the film with droves of happy viewers filling the theaters, despite the fact it had not even been planned for State-side release.

"The three movies I made were not intended for release in the U.S.," Bruce Lee detailed. "They were strictly for the Far East. I had no control over the first two. They are too far out for the Americans. I'm surprised, though they brought in a lot of money for the distributors.

"**Way of the Dragon** was different from the other movies," he added. "We went to Europe for location. The fight scenes between Chuck [Norris] and me were held in the Colosseum in Rome. I also employed a Japanese photographer, because I knew the Japanese had more know-how in that area than those in Hong Kong. This was the

first time a Hong Kong film-maker went to Europe for location shooting. The movie was a little more costly from a Hong Kong standard, but we got our returns right away. Before it even opened, we already sold the distribution rights to Taiwan for the whole production cost."

Lee carefully examined his body of work up until that point and noted, "These films should do for me what the spaghetti westerns did for Clint Eastwood."

He was right, but unbeknownst to anyone, fate was plotting against him.

## THE STORY

Tang Lung (Bruce Lee) arrives in Rome, sent by his uncle to help friends deal with some problems they're having running a restaurant. A syndicate wants the property the restaurant is on and the owner, Chen (a woman), doesn't want to sell. Now the syndicate is starting to apply pressure. Tang reassures her that he can help.

Minor further character definition is achieved when Chen gets him to convert some of his money to the proper currency, and she tries giving him some lessons on trusting people. Then Tang goes to the restaurant to meet everybody and learns that business is awful. He is then led into a back room where the workers are training in karate in order to deal with the syndicate. The students approach Tang and when told that he is an expert at Chinese boxing (kung fu), they insult the form. They demand a demonstration and he agrees, but before they can follow through with it, the chef comes into the back and says they have customers. The camera cuts to the front of the restaurant where representatives from the syndicate are busy chasing customers away. Mr. Ho informs them that if they don't receive a response to their demands by that evening, they will return to tear the place apart.

Evening arrives and people who at first appear to be customers enter the restaurant. They are really from the syndicate and start ripping the place apart, destroying furniture and other items. The workers approach the invaders as Tang merely watches, perhaps assessing the entire situation, planning his potential response.

The fight moves outside of the restaurant and one of the workers is knocked out. Tang finally steps forward and with two great kicks, knocks the assailant unconscious. A second attacker moves forward and falls before the blows of Tang, then a third assailant and finally the fourth. For the moment, victory belongs to the staff of the restaurant.

The next day when told by Chen that anyone in Rome can get a gun, Tang sets about carving darts for reasons he fails to reveal to her. The duo return to the restaurant where a special meal has been made for Tang to thank him for helping them in their fight the day before. Afterwards, the workers get Tang to give them the demonstration they had started. He does so, and they all discard their own karate in favor of Tang's Chinese boxing.

That night, Tang and Chen return to her apartment to be surprised by a man sitting there, with a gun aimed right at them. He wants the two of them to come with him, but Tang doesn't agree and instead uses a dart to disarm the man. He then uses his fighting skills to knock the surprise guest out.

This sequence showed the creativity of writer-director Bruce Lee. Despite what some second rate martial arts movies would have the viewer believe, all the physical training in the world will not stop a bullet. This was an appropriate way of at least *addressing* the idea of an opponent armed in such a way.

The syndicate boss is not pleased over the turn of events when he learns of them. Ho tells him about Tang, emphasizing that he knows kung fu. The gang boss does not see this as a sufficient excuse.

The next morning, Tang eats a breakfast prepared by Chen, who has become infatuated with him from the moment he defended everyone at the restaurant. She says she'll take him on a tour of Rome, which he happily agrees to. At that exact moment, Ho and some syndicate members start beating up the staff of the restaurant in an effort to find out where Tang is.

Next, the camera shows some local color as Chen gives Tang his tour, but he doesn't seem very impressed with what he sees, noting that the Roman ruins look like the ghettos back home. They return to the restaurant, enter and suddenly find themselves held at gunpoint by the syndicate members. The Boss starts slapping Tang's face. Ho places a plane ticket in his pocket and tells him to go back to Hong Kong. The syndicate members lead him outside, the Boss telling them to conceal the gun. When Tang is told to lower his hands so as not to draw attention, he disarms the man with the gun and dispatches the others with an accessible bostaff. The Boss dispatches more people after him, stating, "No guns!" While this works out rather conveniently for Tang, it doesn't make much sense. These guys are ruthless. Surely they've taken lives in the past. Why not now?

The other men, armed with knives, sticks and pipes, reach the alley, where Tang pulls out his nunchukas. A terrific

> **BRUCE LEE'S PUNCH AGAINST A ROMAN SETTING**
> Return of the Dragon, the latest and last (sic) Bruce Lee production, carries the pugilistic punch quite a distance. All the way to Rome, in fact. And in this historic city of ruins, Bruce Lee causes more damage.
> The muscular exponent of sound-effected Chinese boxing inundates the audiences into a suspension of disbelief, pummels a mafia-type gang into a suspension of operation and generally takes such good care of things that even the Italian police can afford a suspension of interference.
> With *Dragon*, Lee has given the boxer film a glossy new image. The European setting is certainly a boost. And Bruce Lee, who also devised the story and wrote the dialogue, has managed to prevent the film from becoming too unbelievably way out. (from the promotional material)

fight scene ensues and no matter how many times the camera has depicted Lee in action, he remains a wonder to behold, his every move indicating a sense of grace in the martial arts.

One of the men picks up a discarded nunchuka and closes with Tang. He swings it once and cracks it into his own head. Tang helps him finish the job. Tang then goes back into the restaurant and uses his darts to disarm two gunmen. This allows the workers to enter the fight, led by Tang. Ho and the Boss attempt a run for the door, but Tang stops them, warning the Boss that if they come back, they'll surely die. Customers begin arriving but a moment later.

At Chen's apartment, she and Tang are talking and she tells him that he has to leave Rome, because they've received word that the syndicate will try to kill him. As this is going on, a sniper's bullet tears into the apartment. Tang sneaks out the door, crosses the street and surreptitiously enters the apartment building. After a little quiet exploration, he finds the right apartment and turns the handle of the door. The would-be assassin empties his pistol into it, and when his gun clicks on an empty chamber, Tang steps in. The man flees and Tang returns to Cheng's apartment to discover that she's missing, taken hostage by the syndicate.

Elsewhere, she's sitting in front of the Boss, who wants her to sign a bill of sale for the restaurant. Tang and workers arrive. Tang disarms the gunmen with his darts. This sequence yet again emphasizes what a creative idea the darts are. Four men surround Tang, but there's no question that he will be victorious. The workers also do prove their abilities in the martial arts, demonstrating what an excellent teacher Tang is. At that moment, Bruce Lee repeats his famous light-shattering kick from **Marlowe**.

Furious, Tang approaches Ho and the Boss. Ho leaps at him with a knife, but quickly backs off. Tang then pushes the Boss into a chair, warning him to back off. Then he leaves. Ho suggests that they call America's best, Colt (Chuck Norris).

At the restaurant everyone is celebrating the Chinese New Year, rejoicing in the lesson they think they've taught the syndicate. Their joy is interrupted by the arrival of Ho, apologizing with a giggle and asking to meet with them the next day. Wong, the leader of the restaurant workers, agrees on everyone's behalf, thinking that this will be a good opportunity for them all to end hostilities and become friends.

Meanwhile, Colt arrives at the airport, while Ho is having to keep a Japanese Hapkido expert and a European karate champion named Bob from destroying each other. They are at odds with each other as to who will receive the honor of killing Tang. A moment later, the Boss and Colt walk in the room, with the Boss saying that Colt is the one who will destroy Tang. As if to prove the wisdom of his decision, he sends the Hapkido expert up against Colt, who quickly knocks the man out.

The next day, Ho meets Tang, Wong and everyone at a restaurant as agreed, but then leads them to an abandoned area into a meeting with the Boss. While there, they're ap-

---

**PROMOTION**

- **DELL PAPERBACK TIE-IN:** Dell books' Legend of Bruce Lee has already sold in excess of one million copies. Contact local book stores for display of posters and stills from Return of the Dragon.
- **BRUCE LEE'S FANS:** Bruce Lee's fans are everywhere and photos of the Kung Fu King from his last movie, Return of the Dragon, will make great giveaways on opening day.
- **CHUCK NORRIS SCHOOLS:** Seven time karate champ, American Chuck Norris, co-stars with Bruce Lee, has karate schools all over the country. Contact them as well as any local school for opening day demonstration at your theatre.
- **FIGHTING STARS MAGAZINE:** The August and September issues of this martial arts magazine devote many pages in full color to Return of the Dragon. Get copies as giveaways and theatre displays.
- **PROMOTE, PROMOTE, PROMOTE:** Bryanston is spending big money in TV, newspapers and radio to bring audiences into your theatre. Combined efforts will make Bruce Lee's Return of the Dragon the biggest Kung Fu hit of them all. (from the promotional booklet)

proached by Bob and the Japanese. Three workers attack them, but are easily beaten. Tang nears Bob and stuns the man with still more impressive kicks, and then sends him into oblivion with a savage punch to the groin. He then turns his attention to the Japanese, who goes down even quicker than Bob did. Ho calls out to Tang to follow him, if he dares. Once Tang disappears in pursuit, Wong stabs two of the restaurant workers, blaming it on Tang. It is now revealed that he is a traitor. Once the restaurant is sold to the syndicate he will have enough money to be established in the life he wants to live, and Tang's interference is jeopardizing that.

Tang follows Ho to the Roman Colosseum (and one has to wonder just how this nice wooded area they had been in leads there), where he sees Colt who gives him the thumbs down sign. At this moment, one can understand Lee's reason for wanting to shoot at this location. It does indeed add a certain epic feel to the proceedings as two great champions face against each other in the ancient arena where so many combats have taken place in the past. An air of tradition hangs heavy over the scene.

Both men obviously know of each other and seem to share a mutual respect. They start limbering up before the inevitable fight. Then the epic conflict begins, obviously a climax to which point much of the film has been prelude. For the first time in his three films, the audience gains a sense that Bruce Lee could actually be in trouble, facing another great martial artist. Tang is knocked down several times and his mouth is bloodied. Then the camera shifts to slow motion for the next portion of the fight sequence, and the technique proves to be a masterful way of demonstrating the power and physical coordination of the fighters. Each of the men punch, kick, parry and never stop dancing around each other. The camera returns to normal speed, and Colt watches the dancing movement of

Tang's feet. Preoccupied, he is kicked by Tang and sent hurtling to the ground. At this moment, it's interesting to note that Lee's "dancing" is similar to the foot motions displayed by former heavyweight boxing champion Muhammad Ali.

Colt gets back on his feet and is knocked down again. Like many of Lee's opponents on film, Colt starts to give in to anger and frustration and *that* always proves to be a fatal mistake. Lee's characters never lose their cool, quiet, compassionless technique, while his opponents often fall prey to hot anger. Tang starts dancing again and Colt tries to imitate him, but the effort fails as Tang switches to a series of lighting punches which send Colt plunging down to the ground yet again.
As the fight continues, Colt's arm and leg are broken, but

## THE LEGEND OF BRUCE LEE

The amazingly talented Bruce Lee has captured the attention of millions of people all over the world. He died at the age of 32 in July 1973, having just completed his own action scenes in what would have been his 5th major film. His last film, which he wrote and directed as well as starred in is **Return of the Dragon**.

Hong Kong could not believe the news of Bruce Lee's sudden death. 120,000 people filled the streets of Kowloon and hundreds more filled the funeral parlor to witness the long processions of friends and film business people paying their last respects to the man they called the "little dragon". Later, Lee's wife and two children accompanied the coffin to Seattle USA where he is buried.

Months were to pass before Britain was aware of the life and death of Bruce Lee. When awareness came, it exploded in an extraordinary way. Fans of Lee range over all ages and classes and have admitted in their letters that they weep at night for him and that they are saving up to visit his grave. Some have devoted a room in their houses as a Bruce Lee room. His likes and dislikes and any other small item of information about him are a matter of absorbing interest for millions of people.

Youngsters, presumably much too young to have seen the R rated Lee films, have written to and telephoned in their thousands for information and pictures of the Kung Fu King.

While **Fists of Fury** was showing at a London West End cinema, the manager discovered one morning that half the front-of-house display was missing. Outdoor posters for **Return of the Dragon** were no sooner exhibited on London display sites than they were carefully removed by someone. An advance lobby board at a cinema had to be covered in plastic to prevent people peeling off the photographs.

Bruce Lee was the rare phenomenon, a superstar. He had the magic ingredient in his personality that film producers would give a king's ransom to be able to predict. No one understands just what it is that makes Bruce Lee the magnetic attraction he is, but his appeal seems likely to last for many years to come. (from the promotional material)

he struggles to his feet. Tang glances at Colt's leg and then shakes his head as if to say, "Look, you've got nothing to prove. Let's stop this while we still can." But Colt is a warrior and there's only one way a battle can end for a warrior: in victory or death. His actions and the setting remind the viewer of the ancient Greco-Roman tradition of the mother advising her warrior son to either return carrying his shield or on it. It is obvious that Colt believes in this tradition. He leaps at Tang, and his neck is broken in the ensuing battle. At this moment, Lee brings forth a great look of frustration, conveying his distaste for this particular victory. He lowers Colt's body to the ground, and covers it with the man's own black belt and uniform top.

This whole sequence is definitely a notch above other films in the martial arts genre, with an understanding silence between the two men more eloquent than words or fisticuffs could ever hope to. Frankly, it's a surprising couple of moments, but indicative of the direction Lee wanted his films to move in.

Ho runs back to Wong, who stabs himself as Tang approaches. Wong tells Tang that they've been betrayed and Tang moves towards Ho. While this is going on, Wong raises his knife and is about to stab Tang, when the Boss pulls up in his car and, apparently fed up with incompetence, shoots Ho, then Wang and attempts to kill Tang, who hides behind a tree. Suddenly the police arrive with Chen and arrest the Boss.

The film ends at the cemetery, where Tang says it's time for him to go. He walks off into the sunset in the tradition of all movie heroes like the Lone Ranger, perhaps looking for the next wrong to right. The tradition extends from the priest Bing Crosby plays in **The Bells of St. Mary** to the lone cowboy assayed by Alan Ladd in **Shane**. Theirs is a lonely life. The hero arrives on the scene, alone, defeats the injustice, and then, just as everyone else is in the midst of happy celebration, departs into the distance.

**Return of the Dragon** serves as an impressive debut performance for Bruce Lee as a writer and director in addition to serving as actor and choreographer. His choice of adding non-Chinese cast members and European locales definitely helped to broaden the film's appeal.

Still, the production also brings with it a certain sense of repetition from **Fists of Fury** and **The Chinese Connection** in that Lee portrays a man who joins family members in a business and/or karate school, and then leads them into battle against oppressors. Many of his comrades are killed and he must avenge their deaths. Changes, however, are wrought in that the Boss is arrested at the end and Lee is not held responsible for any deaths. There is also some real emotion displayed in key sequences, particularly during the fight scene between Bruce Lee and Chuck Norris. Norris, of course, is the martial artist and teacher who would go on to star in a series of his own films continuing into the 1990s.

One thing **Return of the Dragon** *did* prove was that if Bruce Lee was going to achieve his goal of being a world famous martial arts star, then an American production was what he needed.

And that's what he found in **Enter the Dragon**.

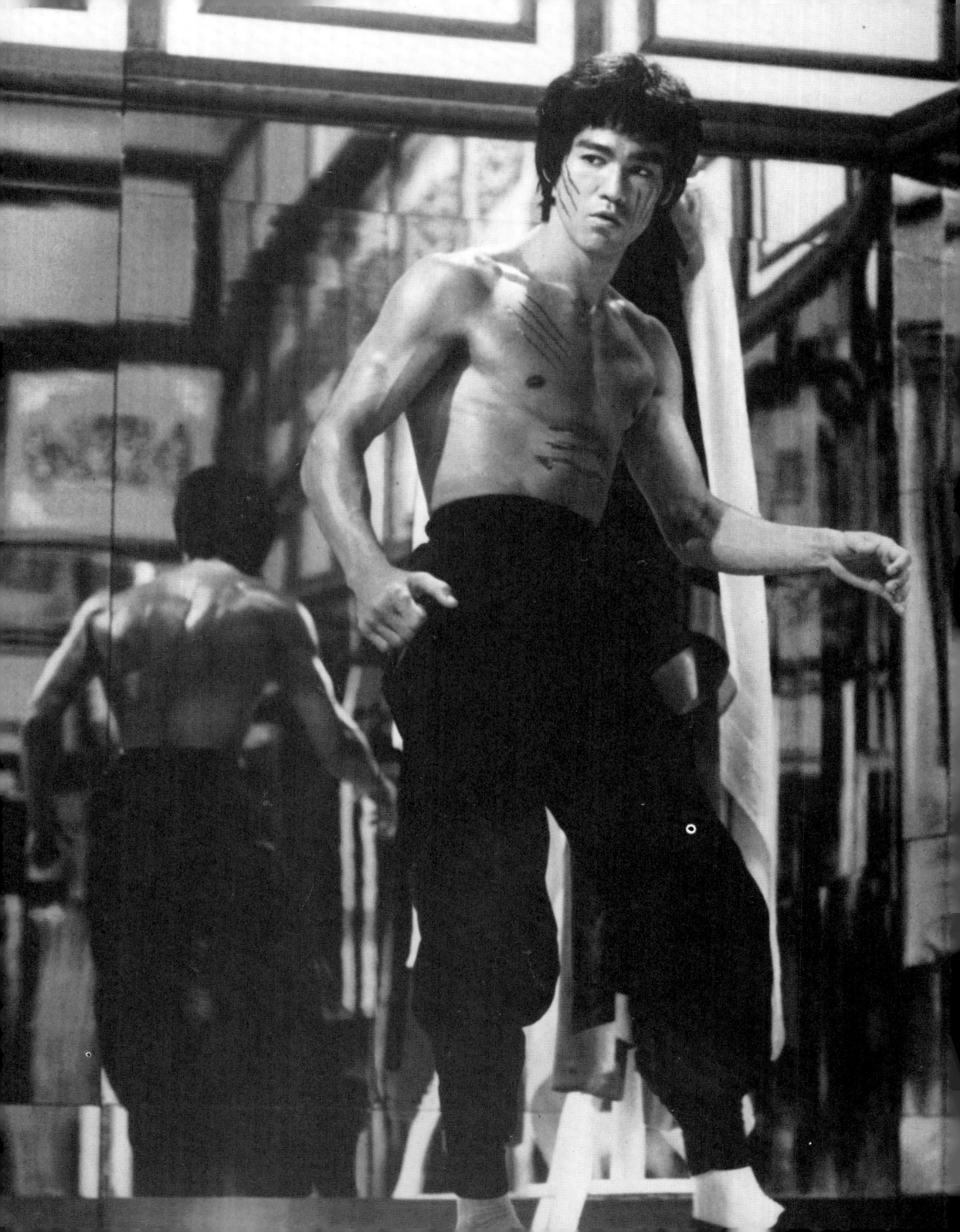

## CAST

Bruce Lee: Lee

John Saxon: Roper

Jim Kelly: Williams

Ahna Capri: Tania

Bob Wall: Oharra

Shih Kien: Han

Angela Mao Ying: Su-Lin

Betty Chung: Mei Ling

Geoffrey Weeks: Braithwaite

Yang Sze: Bolo

Peter Archer: Parsons

## CREDITS

Producers: Fred Weintraub & Paul Hiller

In Association With Raymond Chow

Director: Robert Clouse

Written by Michael Allin

Director of Photography: Gilbert Hubbs

Set Supervisor: Wong Sun

Film Editors: Kurt Hirshler & George Watters

Property Master: Wong Shun Chong

Sound Mixer: Zee Shao Lin

Fight Sequences Staged by Bruce Lee

Music Editor: Gene Marks

Music: Lalo Schifrin

A Warner Brothers Release

# Fists Of Fury

MPAA Rating: R
Running Time: 98 Minutes

## BEHIND THE SCENES

"I think Bruce had an enormous impact upon the emerging of the martial arts in the film industry," Warner Brothers executive Ted Ashley detailed in a *Black Belt* magazine tribute to Lee. "Clearly, the first of the martial arts pictures to break in the United States was one that we happened to put out, *Five Fingers of Death*, which was very successful. Two of the Chinese-language films made by Bruce were released very shortly thereafter and helped enormously to solidify the appetite for martial arts films. Bruce's contribution was even more definitive in **Enter the Dragon**. The movie blended the best of the martial arts film-making with other qualities and production values which brought the film, the world of martial arts and Bruce Lee to a much wider audience."

Without a doubt, **Enter the Dragon** was Bruce Lee's dream film project come true. He was able to take his vast knowledge of the martial arts and film-making, and apply it to an American production, which was the first of its kind.

Much of the initial credit for this project must go to Ashley as well as the film's producers, Fred Weintraub and Paul Heller, who never doubted that it would work.

"If it wasn't for Ted Ashley," Weintraub once explained, "the movie would never have gotten made. I had half the money, but everybody else had turned me down—including other executives at Warners.

"I had seen **The Big Boss** and I thought [Bruce] was sensational in it. So I went to Hong Kong to see him and met

Raymond Chow. We put together a deal which we were going to do with their company [Golden Harvest] in mind. Then after I came back, Warner Brothers got interested and decided to become a partner...Ted asked me what I needed, then said, 'Go ahead.'"

The project came together fairly quickly, although Lee himself nearly held things up a bit, due to what Weintraub felt was the enormous pressure of tackling such a project.

In *The Bruce Lee Story* Weintraub noted, "Bruce was undoubtedly nervous, even apprehensive about **Enter the Dragon**. A lot was riding on it—it was his first big international film. Then, of course, he was on his home ground and I think he wanted to avoid giving the impression of partiality toward Americans by favoring them at the expense of his own ethnic group. So there was the dichotomy operating for him. And on the whole, he wanted the film to be more Chinese than American, which was very understandable. About our differences—well, first, the script

---

**BRUCE LEE BRINGS BACK THAT GOLDEN AGE OF MOVIE MAKING**

The big karate experts have long known what it means to be busy, honored and feared, but one thing their skill didn't bring them was a lush style of living. Muscular young Bruce Lee gave a new look to that proud profession. Bruce had a huge home with 11 beautiful bedrooms and when it was time to do his thing, he would speed off in his special Rolls-Royce. His untimely death in July of this year was a great loss, not only to motion pictures, but also to the world of the martial arts.

In less than two years, Lee starred in three action movies that made the martial arts one of the hottest things ever to hit the screen. The newest and biggest Bruce Lee film in which he plays a James Bondian secret agent is **Enter the Dragon**.

The fact that Warner Brothers wanted to produce **Enter the Dragon** is a reflection of the unparalleled international success Bruce Lee's martial arts movies enjoyed. Originally aimed at the karate fans of the Far East, these explosive action dramas are now major box office attractions around the globe.

For that reason, producers Fred Weintraub and Paul M. Heller brought together talents from the Orient, the United States and Europe for their king-size cast. Co-starred with Lee, Saxon and Miss Capril are Jim Kelly, 1971 International Middleweight Karate Champion, and Bob Wall, 1970 Professional Karate Champion.

Though born in San Francisco, Bruce Lee started his screen career as a child actor in Hong Kong-made Chinese-language films. He began studying karate when he was quite young and mastered that art so well that Hollywood's TV producers soon grabbed him for featured parts. Hong Kong movie magnate Raymond Chow saw Bruce's work and sensing that he was meant for something bigger, he signed him for his first starring role in **Fists of Fury**, a picture that broke all box office records in Hong Kong. He followed swiftly with **The Chinese Connection** and **Return of the Dragon**, the latter also written and directed by Lee. Those three pictures grossed $3.5 million in Singapore and Hong Kong alone. Their success in Asia was immense, but their success in Europe and America was overwhelming.

Filmed on location in Hong Kong, with additional scenes shot in Los Angeles and San Francisco, **Enter the Dragon** was directed by Robert Clouse. The screenplay was written by Michael Allin, and is the first martial arts movie to be filmed in English and the first to be made by an American film company. (from the promotional material)

could never have been to his liking. He and the writer just didn't see eye-to-eye. It took us two to three weeks before Bruce finally showed up...I just went ahead and shot sequences, even though Bruce wasn't ready to star. I kept telling Warner Brothers he was going to show up every day—for Linda had told me that eventually he would. Eventually he did.

"I think he was kind of hibernating in those first few weeks. I think he was terribly frightened. Here he had this big chance—and there's no question that he would have been the biggest superstar had he lived, for he had this thing that happens to great performers on screen—it's a kind of magnetism. It's the same with guys like Clint Eastwood—just a nice guy when you meet him at a party, but something unique and special when he gets on the screen...It was not easy for him—and I don't think anybody can be glib about it. You can't dismiss it as ego-tripping or anything like that. Here he was, the greatest martial artist-actor of them all, lining up as it were, for the Olympics. It was the big moment—all he had been striving for."

**Enter the Dragon** was shot in Hong Kong and the United States, and used a crew from both countries. The approach was to take a Chinese production and make it with American film techniques.

"I'd seen all the old Japanese pictures," Weintraub explained in *The Legendary Bruce Lee*. "I thought most were too stylized and much too long. They were great ideas, but much too formal and ritualistic. It was only in the last 20 minutes after three hours of preaching and philosophy that the hero would face off against a dozen men and emerge victorious. That was the exciting part—if you were still awake by that time. The hero was always a superman type. I believe in film heroes. I'm tired of the star being a slob."

Weintraub believed that the martial arts film was akin to a deadly type of ballet, while not apologizing for the inherent violence. "It's a violent world," he'd noted at the time. "We don't pretend to be trying to reform people through films, and we don't believe film violence contributes to real violence. In any event, it's entertainment and that's what we are interested in giving people."

Added co-producer Paul Heller, "A guy who goes to see this film can once again feel that maybe he too can change his life for the better: right wrongs, improve things for everyone. Despite the violence in the film, there is the net positive good. The lone hero is a great and traditional kind of story that's particularly American. And even though **Enter the Dragon** was of an Oriental subject, its basic theme was thoroughly American in attitude."

Robert Clouse, a veteran action film director, was the perfect choice for the film. The casting of Americans John Saxon as Roper and Jim Kelly as Williams, Lee's allies in the film, seemed almost providential. But it was Bruce Lee himself who was going to make or break the film, as he was the creative force behind the choreography of the various

---

## SCREEN IDEAS MUST PASS TEST

"When I get a new idea, I go to sleep and try to forget it. If I'm still hooked when I wake up, I start doing it."

That candid confession comes from Fred Weintraub, and the ideas he has had have brought him great success—in advertising, in the music world and, most recently, in moviemaking.

The latest idea to pass the test took Weintraub (and a talented film crew) from Hollywood to Hong Kong. The motion picture they made there for Warner Brothers is **Enter the Dragon**, the first martial arts adventure to come from a major studio.

Thinking of things to put on the screen was what brought Fred Weintraub to Hollywood four years ago. It's hard to name a man with such an endlessly active mind. Warner Brothers solved it by calling him the Creative Vice President. Before that title had been embossed on his wall, he brought to the company Woodstock, one of the biggest bonanzas in its fifty-year history.

Weintraub has been alert to the growing interest in the martial arts for some time. Three years ago he developed the Kung Fu story which has now become one of the most successful current television series. Weintraub's rush into Hong Kong to shoot **Enter the Dragon** is typical of his style. Waste no time turning an idea into an event.

Thanks largely to Weintraub's booming enthusiasm, Warner Brothers is the first company to use Hollywood-style in dramatizing those Asian arts. (from the promotional material)

fights, and they were indeed spectacular. No special effects were needed to enhance his abilities. In fact Clouse stated, "If we'd shot him at regular speed it would have blurred. Incredible is the only word I can use. He is a phenomenon."

**Enter the Dragon**, as everyone connected with the film had believed, opened to tremendous box office around the world, firmly establishing Bruce Lee as one of filmdom's most popular superstars, transcending the genre and any martial artist who had come before him. And eclipsing any who were to follow.

"This is the movie I'm proud of," Lee exclaimed, "because it is made for the U.S. audience as well as for the European and Oriental. This is definitely the biggest movie I ever made. I'm excited to see what happens."

Unfortunately, he never did.

## THE STORY

Lee (Bruce Lee) is in the midst of a martial arts demonstration at a Shaolin Temple, defeating an opponent with hardly any effort. Later, he is greeted by Braithwaite (Geoffrey Weeks), a member of an intelligence agency, who discusses a tournament run by someone named Han. Lee has been invited to it, but has refused to enter.

Before they can continue their discussion, Lee excuses himself, as it is time for him to instruct a student. As the lesson begins, we are offered a dose of Lee's philosophy of becoming one with the universe. This does not come across as heavy-handed, due to the humor of the sequence.

The film cuts to the main credits and the wonderful Lalo Schifrin theme, as Roper (John Saxon) and Williams (Jim Kelly) arrive in Hong Kong. The credits come to an end, and Lee is shown sitting in a room with Braithwaite,

watching the only available film footage of Han, who was once a member of Lee's temple. Han is now considered a renegade. Lee also observes Han's facially scarred bodyguard, Oharra (Bob Wall). Lee is told that if he accepts this request, he will use the guise of the tournament to get onto Han's island, which is heavily fortified. Han is completely self-sufficient, his only contact with the outside world a tournament he holds once every three years. Han refers to the island as his school of martial arts, but there's much more to it than that. The body of a woman who had been on his private junk was found, and it is the agency's belief that Han lures beautiful women to the island, lures them into becoming dependent on drugs and then sells them into slavery.

They need Lee to gather enough firsthand evidence on Han's operation to give them grounds to arrest him. In addition, Braithwaite states that agent Mei Ling had infiltrated the island, but there's been no word from her. If he finds her, perhaps she will be able to enlighten him. Lee wants to know why somebody just doesn't blow Han's brains out. He's

---

**KELLY'S KARATE IS NOT FAKED**

Jim Kelly's latest chance to show his way with the martial arts is in **Enter the Dragon**, which introduces (him) and stars Bruce Lee, John Saxon and the beautiful Ahna Capri. A very rugged and bright young black who comes from Kentucky, Jim has done better than well at karate. He won the International Middleweight Championship in 1971 and is one of the leading instructors of that art in Los Angeles.

In **Enter the Dragon** Jim hunts for a warlord of international crime who disguises his island fortress as a martial arts academy. Kelly's role called for him to fight such martial arts masters as Peter Archer, 1971 Commonwealth Karate Champion, and Shih Kien, a noted Hong Kong black belt and hapkido teacher.

Despite his booming movie career, Jim Kelly is still hooked hard on karate—off or on the screen.

There are seasoned moviemakers who expect that Jim Kelly will grow into a film fixture, handling a variety of roles. But for the foreseeable future, expect to focus on his leaping legs and iron-like arms.

One of the great things about seeing Jim Kelly on the screen is that none of his rough stuff has even a touch of make-believe. The opponent he reaches at the end of a seven foot leap is actually feeling an angry human leg. And when Jim himself is decked down to the floor, his wincing shoulder knows it's for real. No matter how demanding a fight, Jim Kelly never uses a stunt double.

"I like the dramatic part of acting, the talking and the emotional things," Jim will tell you. "But the karate has to be karate. What the hell, that's the world I come from."

*(from the promotional material)*

told in response that after an assassination attempt some time ago, Han has become completely paranoid, and will allow no guns on the island.

Lee ultimately agrees, as in flashback we learn that three years earlier, Oharra was involved in the death of his sister, Su Lin (Angela Mao). This flashback is handled quite well, as Su Lin, a hapkido black belt, fights off and tries to elude Oharra—whose face she scars—and his men. Their pursuit of her is quite suspenseful, the helplessness of her plight driven home by an elderly woman who witnesses the entire tragedy, but merely closes her window, choosing not to become involved. The sequence culminates in Oharra cornering Su Lin at a warehouse, where she kills herself with a shard of broken glass rather than allow the men to defile her. Flashback ended, Lee visits the grave of his mother, and apologizes to her spirit, stating that going to Han's island is something that he *must* do.

Meanwhile, on his way to Han's junk, there is a flashback in which we learn that Roper suffers tremendous debt, owing a loan shark nearly $200,000. Goons show up to make sure he's fully aware of the debt, but he quickly dispatches them with karate moves. The tournament on Han's island is his only way to get the money he needs.

Williams' flashback reveals that he was accosted by police simply because he's black, but as in the case with Roper, he manages to remove the problem and continues on his way. He gets to the junk, where it is shown that he and Roper are old friends.

On the junk, another champion, Parsons, starts to abuse one of the Orientals and then approaches Lee, demanding to know what style he represents. "The art of fighting without fighting," Lee replies and then tricks Parsons into getting in a row boat and tugging him along behind the vessel.

They arrive on Han's island and it becomes very clear it is indeed a fortress. An overhead shot establishes hundreds of karate students in training. This shot adds much to the film; one of the problems detractors often note of kung fu films is that *everyone* is fully versed in the martial arts, an obviously very unrealistic portrayal. At least in this case, there is a perfectly logical explanation for it, which adds a realism to the proceedings.

Later, they are all given a taste of Han's lifestyle, an Oriental version of what most Americans assume life at the Playboy Mansion must be like. There is ample food, riotous partying and beautiful, and willing, women. In the midst of these festivities, Han (Shih Kien) greets everyone, thanks them for coming and expresses his gratitude.

Later, the men are given their choice of women for the night. Lee chooses Mei Ling, the planted agent. When they're alone, he begins pumping her for information. All she can tell him—and it's something he already knows—is that women come to the island and disappear.

The next morning, Lee attends a training session which serves a a prelude to the tournament. Han takes his place on what can only be described as a throne, overseeing the

---

## JOHN SAXON IS KARATE STUDENT

John Saxon has been a popular film and television actor for many years, but until his starring performance in Warner Brothers' **Enter the Dragon**, it was not generally known that Saxon was a long time student of the ancient Oriental martial arts of karate and tai chi chuan.

"At first I rejected the idea of doing a film involving the martial arts," Saxon admits. "I wanted to keep my training a private thing. My greatest apprehension was exploiting the martial arts in a movie."

Saxon changed his mind when he learned that **Enter the Dragon** would feature several of the world's greatest martial arts champions. Saxon stars in the international adventure with Bruce Lee, the most famous martial arts film star of all, who in 1972 was elected to the Black Belt Hall of Fame.

While he was studying the art of acting, Saxon, who had been a serious athlete as a youth, became involved in the martial arts. He studied judo and then karate. But as he began to act more frequently, he found that he didn't have time to devote to them.

In 1966 he discovered tai chi chuan. "It was fascinating to me because it looked exactly like the psycho physical exercises I'd recently learned in an acting class." Saxon began studying the ancient Chinese defensive art and found that it helped him as an actor. "Tai chi was almost the exact equivalent of the acting exercise." (from the promotional material)

events much like an Emperor overseeing his gladiators in Ancient Rome.

In the first match, Williams proves victorious over Parsons. One important aspect of the staging of this fight is its incredible, and difficult to achieve on-screen, realism. The blows seem to actually strike, although the sound effects, at times, are hard to believe. This is in strong contrast to the majority of king fu films, where limbs sometimes flail without rhyme or reason, and the sound effects occasionally indicate that wind can be smashed wind with a hand.

Roper is next to fight in a match, and he appears to be losing badly, though he ultimately dispatches his opponent by striking just a wee bit below the belt.

That night, Williams goes for a walk on the island, while Lee sets out in search of answers. What Lee finds is a system of underground caverns. Just as he is about to explore them, his search is interrupted by several guards, who he is forced to deal with. After the incident, he returns to his room.

The next morning, a rather displeased Han states that someone sought diversion on the grounds, but he points out that the identity of that person is not important at the moment. What *is* important is that his guards failed in their duty, and all are killed by Bolo (Yan Sze) as a lesson while everyone watches.

This sad duty completed, the tournament begins in earnest. Lee faces Oharra, and as he raises his hands, there's a quick cut to the image of Su Lin raising the shard of glass, ready to plunge it into her abdomen—a splendidly handled moment on film—after which Lee strikes out. Oharra is sent crashing to the ground. He falls again two more times, and then tries to knock Lee down by pulling at his leg. Instead Lee performs a back-flip culminating with both his

feet smashing into Oharra's face (a wonderfully visual stunt!). Furious, Oharra leaps at him, but Lee drops, delivers a kick to Oharra's stomach before both return to their feet again. The angrier Oharra gets, the less he is able to do against his opponent, a point which once again emphasizes Lee's philosophy of mind over emotion. It was a philosophy utilized to great effect in the first two *Karate Kid* films as well.

Desperate, Oharra breaks a bottle and tries to stab Lee with the jagged edge, but fails. At that moment, Lee extracts revenge for for the death of his sister, killing Oharra. Han's only reaction is to comment that Oharra's treachery has disgraced them all. The tournament ends for the moment.

At that time, Williams is summoned to Han's study, where he is congratulated by Han for the fighting skills he demonstrated the previous day. Then Han accuses him of being the one to attack his guards. Williams replies that he wasn't the only one on the grounds the previous night. Han demands to know who the intruder was and, at that point, several students enter the room.

"Man," Williams sneers, perhaps winking at the audience, "you come right out of a comic book!"

The men move in for the kill, but Williams quickly dispatches them. Then the film proceeds to a logical conclusion as an all out fist-fest between Williams and Han begins. They both crash through a wall and into an opium den, where Han uses steel hands to pummel his opponent.

Later, Han gives Roper a tour of his museum and they observe a variety of *hands*, including both a steel-clawed one and a human skeletal one, which Han deems a "souvenir"—definitely a wonderfully bizarre touch. At this point, it becomes even more clear Han is a villain very much modeled after the antagonist in a James Bond film. He lives on his own fortified isolated island and collects steel hands ala Dr. No in the film of the same name. He even strokes a white cat, perhaps the most commonly associated image of an 007 villain, an image firmly established by Ernst Stavro Blofeld.

They move underground, where Han shows Roper the island's power plant, and then introduces him to his "daughters", who are also his personal guards. The tour continues and Roper sees Han's opium-making operation, and wonders why Han is exposing so much to him. The reason becomes obvious when he asks Roper to join his organization as a U.S. representative. Roper starts to understand the reason for the tournaments: it's an ideal way to recruit new talent.

> **PROMOTIONS NATIONAL MAGAZINE EXPOSURE**
>
> As an example of the intense interest aroused by Enter the Dragon, the August issue of Esquire carries an indepth story on the film and Bruce Lee. In addition, the August issue of Black Belt, the world's leading magazine of self-defense, carries a full color cover showing John Saxon in action and a five page inside story, illustrated with scenes from the film. (from the promotional materi[al])

They continue walking and pass cells with numerous prisoners. Han dismisses them as refuse from waterfront bars (and there never is any further explanation, which is a bit of a shortcoming of the film). These prisoners remain eerily silent as they exchange stares with Roper.

A moment later, Roper becomes horrified to see Williams' corpse in chains before it is dropped into a vat of acid. Han explains that he was forced to ask Williams questions to which there were no answers. Roper seethes with hatred for the man, which intensifies when Han says that he wants him to be aware of the realities of serving the organization.

Meanwhile, Lee makes his way back to the underground. Lee disposes of several guards and passes glass walled cells with captive beautiful women inside. One woman appears in a completely dazed state, while the other pleads with him to help her. Lee has no choice but to continue, as he finds his way to the island's radio transmitter and signals Braithwaite. Lee accomplishes this by placing a poisonous snake he found earlier in the booth, forcing the operators to leap through the window to safety. A moment after his transmission has been completed, an alarm sounds and Lee is forced to go into action.

What follows is a veritable ballet of a fight sequence, as Lee starts eliminating approaching guards, first one and then two at a time. The number of guards continually increases and yet Lee handles them all, eventually using a bostaff and a nunchuka. Describing each movement would be impossible, but suffice to say that Bruce Lee is absolutely incredible. This sequence serves as the only proof needed to understand the incredible popularity of this martial artist/actor at the time. This is one of *the* best fight scenes ever shot for a martial arts film.

> **MARTIAL ARTS SCHOOLS MAJOR SOURCE FOR SPECIAL PROMOTIONS**
>
> An exciting and highly visual promotion would be to hold martial arts demonstrations at the theatre. Arrange to have teams of martial artists in full fighting gear show their techniques on your stage, in the lobby or on the sidewalk in front of the theatre, if local laws permit. Be sure to provide a p.a. system and invite a local deejay or sports personality to carry the commentary.
>
> In addition, try to set up a demonstration in a public place such as a park, a beach, a playground or the parking lot of a shipping center. Naturally, a full complement of one sheets and other display material should be utilized.
>
> Also, you could try to promote free courses by making a tie-up with a local martial arts school. These courses could be given away as prizes in a radio contest or any other special promotion. (from the promotional material)

Disposing of the last guard, Lee finds himself trapped in a small chamber. The next morning at the tournament, Han asks Roper to take part in the morning's "edification". He pits Roper against Lee in a fight, but Roper refuses to face this opponent. Han instead sends in a wall of a man named Bolo to fight Roper. Lee is about to enter the fight against the new opponent, but Roper restrains him, indicating that he wishes to face his attacker alone. Lee accepts this request, and steps back. While this is going on, Mei Ling enters the underground passages and begins to free the prisoners. Meanwhile top-side, the fight continues to rage. After a lengthy exchange of blows, Roper ultimately defeats Bolo.

John Saxon handles himself well in this scene, but it's difficult to believe his movements could have destroyed someone like Bolo. The audience doesn't have much time to ponder this deficiency, as a furious Han dispatches more of his students into the arena, where they battle Lee and Roper. Here the camera almost lovingly dwells on Lee, and once again it is a sight to behold. The performer is sensational!

Soon all the students are involved, but our heroes are helped by the now-released prisoners who partake in what has essentially become a brawl. Han, thinking only of survival, removes a steel hand and replaces it with an animal-like claw. He slashes Lee's face, drawing blood. As we've seen in earlier movies of Bruce Lee, he doesn't take kindly to such a thing. The fight continues for a few seconds, until Han's claw becomes imbedded in a piece of wood. Then a blow from Lee separates him from the appendage. Before Lee can close with his opponent, he is distracted by another fighter. Han uses this opportunity to escape to his museum, where he removes a much deadlier

---

### "WOW", "POW", AND "OW" THEM WITH SOUND-EFFECTS RECORD

There's a great way to get into a funny tie-up with a local deejay. It's a record made from the actual sound effects in the movie—the grunts and groans, the oh's and ah's, the kicks and chops and falls that dominate the track and add so much to *Enter the Dragon*. To enable you to get a lot of mileage out of this disc, Warner Brothers has prepared a sheet of verbal cues for use on a radio show. Introduced by one or more of the cues, the 40-second disc should get considerable interest from listeners—the kind of reaction that might well lead to another airing on that station or another one.

A good place to use the disc is your own lobby, via the p.a. system. Patrons going in and out would be tickled by the array of strange and funny sounds. But be sure to put up a sign telling them what they're listening to. (form the promotional material)

claw-hand from its display and attaches it to his wrist.

Lee suddenly appears. "You have offended my family. You have offended the Shaolin Temple," he says.

The fight has descended to a more personal level as their battle begins anew. A pair of mid-air leaps allows Han to slash Lee's stomach and shoulder. He tastes the blood and becomes thoroughly angered. One incredible kick actually knocks Han out of the film frame in such a way as to be completely startling to the viewer.

Han escapes, but is tracked to a room of mirrors. There a highly suspenseful game of cat and mouse ensues. This is terrific filmwork; neither Han nor Lee are able to tell which image is the real one and which is but a mirrored reflection. Han occasionally leaps out, slashes Lee and "vanishes" again. Lee spots the real Han and delivers a side-kick which sends him flying. This is beautifully shot with multi-imaging of Han's body showing him flying by a wall of mirrors as Lee pursues him.

Becoming frustrated with this game of death, Lee starts smashing the mirrors, eliminating Han's hiding places. Finally, as the viewer always knows it must, it is just the two of them, with no outside distractions. Lee impales Han on a spear that the man had previously tried to kill him with. At the close of this sequence, as the hero leaves the room via a rotating wall, director Robert Clouse presents a splendid shot of Han's body, still impaled on the wall, spinning in and out of frame, his death symbolically captured in the room of broken mirrors for all eternity.

Interestingly, as much as **Enter the Dragon** draws obvious influences from the Bond films, it also proved to have lasting impact on the world of 007. *The Man With the Golden Gun* offered a very strong kung fu slant with the film culminating in a battle between Bond and villain Scaramanga in a house of mirrors.

Lee returns to the surface, where Roper and the former prisoners have proven victorious, although there seems to be little glory in victory. Lee and Roper share a thumbs up sign, indicating that everything's okay. Or, at least, the best they can hope for under the circumstances. At that moment, Braithwaine's people arrive via helicopter, and Lee's look seems to indicate, "Why bother?"

The camera locks on Han's clawed hand and the credits roll.

The last ten minutes of the film contain no dialogue, allowing the action and the camera be most eloquent.

**Enter the Dragon** is one hell of a good action/kung fu film. For the most part, everyone does a great job, although Lee, the superstar, stands out. The man deserved every bit of recognition he received and one can only imagine the body of work he would have left behind had he lived longer. As it is, we can only conjecture.

**Game of Death** not withstanding, this was an appropriate send-off for his fans. It was as though the Little Dragon, like the Lone Ranger, had righted the wrongs he set himself upon, and then rode off into the sunset.

And we never even got a chance to thank him!

## PRODUCTION NOTES

Two leading American moviemakers, China's most popular action star and a popular American film and television star have come together in Hong Kong, bringing a fresh look to those roaringly successful films about the martial arts. The American producers are Fred Weintraub and Peter M. Heller. The stars are Bruce Lee and John Saxon. The explosive drama of today's martial arts is **Enter the Dragon**, which also stars Ahna Capri and introduces Jim Kelly.

The martial arts of Asia are man-to-man styles of fighting,

which run the gamut from very rugged sports to deadly combat. They include karate, hapkido, kung fu and judo.

Recently, screen dramas tied to the martial arts have become enormously popular around the world. **Enter the Dragon** marks the first time that a major American film company has gone to Hong Kong, birthplace of martial arts movies, to make an international martial arts film. The huge cast engaged by producers Weintraub and Heller unites the talents of the United States, Europe and the Orient.

Bruce Lee was a major factor in the international success earned by martial arts motion pictures. His uncommon combination of great physical strength, fine looks and real acting style made him the top martial arts film star. In **Enter the Dragon**, Lee stars as a James Bond-type super secret agent drawn into combat with a clever crim-

---

## THE ANCIENT MARTIAL ARTS COME TO LIFE IN ENTER THE DRAGON

In **Enter the Dragon** three great actor-martial artists perform astounding feats of strength and dexterity. The three, Bruce Lee, who was Asia's top martial arts film star; John Saxon, American television and film star and karate expert; and Jim Kelly, 1971 International Middleweight Karate Champion, practice some of the varieties of the ancient Oriental arts of fighting self-defense. These are ancient disciplines which today are being practiced by hundreds of thousands of Americans.

The martial arts developed over many centuries from several varieties of Chinese boxing. Known under the general name "kung fu" Chinese boxing is probably the world's oldest sport, after hunting. It is certainly the world's oldest formal system of self-defense. The earliest references to it date from the fourteenth century before Christ.

During the ensuing centuries numerous varieties of martial arts developed in the Orient. Different countries became identified with different styles: China (kung fu), Korea (tai kwan do), Japan (karate). The sudden surge of interest in these arts has confronted many Americans with an array of unfamiliar terms. This glossary is designed to clarify some of them.

KARATE, a highly respected discipline in Japan, means "empty hands". It is a style of fighting considered by practitioners to be an art form. Karate primarily involves the use of the hands, legs being used mainly for tripping. Participants are expected to keep on their feet.

JUDO: A sport derived from Ju Jitsu. In Ju Jitsu everything goes; break a man's arm, gouge out his eyes, Asia, discourage major injuries. Ju Jitsu is relegated to the category of back alley revenge.

TAI KWON DO: The Korean form of Karate, which uses dynamic kicks more than hand plots.

TAI CHI CHUAN: The Chinese art of overcoming an opponent by yielding to his attack and defeating him by catching him off balance.

KENDO: A sport which finds its roots in the ancient techniques of Samurai sword fighting. In Kendo, the participants use bamboo sticks instead of swords and fight with masks and padding in much the same way that fencers do.

HAPKIDO: A form of Karate which calls for grappling and kicking. It was seen in the Warner Brothers release Billy Jack.

In addition to Lee, Saxon and Kelly, **Enter the Dragon** features many prominent martial artists. Among them are Bob Wall, 1970 United States Professional Karate Champion; Yan Sze, Shotokan Championship of Southeast Asia; Angela Mao Ying, Black Belt Hapkido champion of Okinawa; plus more than 200 other martial artists from around the world. (from the promotional material)

inal who uses a martial arts academy to mask a career of international crime.

John Saxon, who stars with Lee, portrays a rugged American who becomes Bruce's brother in battle. His screen credits include *The Appaloosa, Joe Kidd* and *House Made of Dawn*. He has marked successes in "The Doctors" portion of the TV series *The Bold Ones*, and he recently starred in a stage production of *Guys and Dolls*.

Ahna Capri, who first gained fame in Germany as a magazine model, co-stars as an international beauty who is the mistress of a sinister island fortress. Ahna comes to Hollywood from Europe after several seasons in the theatre in New York. On the screen, Ahna has starred in *Payday, Brotherhood of Satan* and opposite Rod Taylor in *Darker Than Amber*.

Jim Kelly, a handsome sinewy black youth whose chief profession up to now has been karate fighter and teacher, co-stars as a martial arts expert who jets in from Los Angeles to participate in a deadly martial arts competition. Kelly, the 1971 International Middleweight Karate Champion, is also a sports star in track, baseball and football.

The production team of Weintraub and Heller brought many years of entertainment experience to **Enter the Dragon**. Both have held executive positions at Warner Brothers and have impressive production credits. Weintraub helped bring the fabulously successful *Woodstock* to the screen and he produced *Rage*, which starred and was directed by George C. Scott. Heller supervised the development of such equally important pictures as *Dirty Harry* and *Skin Game*,

Robert Clouse, who directed **Enter the Dragon** from a screenplay by Michael Allin, has earned Academy Award nominations for two films shorts which he wrote, directed and produced—*Cadillac* and *Jimmy Blue Eyes*. His first feature directing assignments were *Dreams of Glass* and *Darker Than Amber*.

The cast of **Enter the Dragon**, the largest ever used for a movie of the martial arts, spent three months filming in and around Hong Kong and California. Locations included Kowloon, a floating sampan city, Victoria Harbor, Hong Kong Island, Los Angeles and San Francisco. The film was produced in association with Raymond Chow of Hong Kong's Concorde Productions.(from the promotional material)

## EYE-CATCHING STICK-ON LABELS

The young crowd is crazy about labels. You can turn this craze to your advantage and stir up advance interest for **Enter the Dragon**. These are bright yellow with black imprinting and are pressure-sensitive for easy stick-on. When seen on a person, the words **Enter the Dragon** are certain to stimulate questions, curiosity and, ultimately, word-of-mouth. Distribute in your lobby prior to playdate; tie-up with a radio station and have D.J.'s offer the labels to listeners; pass them out in shopping areas and other places where they will get full exposure. (from the promotional material)

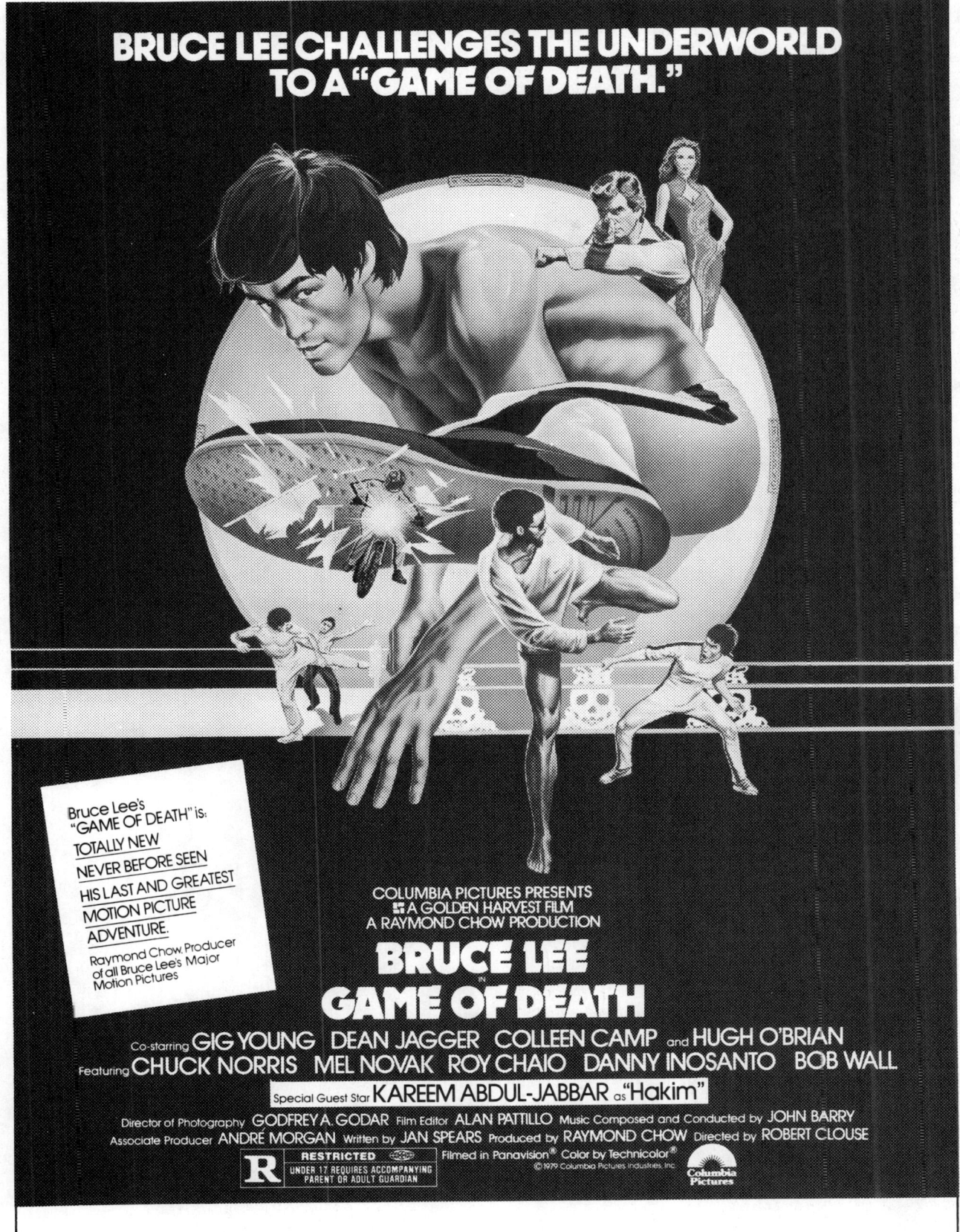

## CAST

Billy Lo: Bruce Lee
Jim Marshall: Gig Young
Dr. Land: Dean Jagger
Steiner: Hugh O'Brian
Ann Morris: Colleen Camp
Carl Miller: Robert Wall
Stick: Mel Novak
Hakim: Kareem Abdul-Jabbar
Fighter: Chuck Norris
Pasqual: Danny Inosanto

## CREDITS

Produced by Raymond Chow
Directed by Robert Clouse
Written by Jan Spears
Director of Photography: Godfrey A. Godar
Film Editor: Alan Pattillo
Music Composed & Conducted by John Barry
Associate Producer: Andre: Morgan
Released From Columbia Pictures
MPAA Rating: R
Running Time: 102 Minutes

## BEHIND THE SCENES

Bruce Lee's proposed follow-up to **Enter the Dragon** was ironically entitled **Game of Death**. The irony became all too obvious on July 20, 1973 when it was announced that the martial arts master, innovative actor and idol of millions worldwide had died.

The passing of a Cary Grant or a Laurence Olivier can generally be accepted by their fans, as they had lived long lives and left a stunning film legacy. On the other hand, the James Dean's, Marilyn Monroe's or John Lennon's who are taken away with an unexpected abruptness, leave a void in their wake. It was into this unfortunate category that Bruce Lee fell. Over the course of several years he had moved to the threshold of being the new Eastwood, Bronson or Reynolds. Suddenly it was all gone. His fans were shocked, and refused to believe that their hero had left them.

Rumors abounded. Some suggested foul play, others a drug overdose. The most widely accepted explanation was a brain hemorrhage, supposedly brought about by being struck in the head so many times throughout his career. Linda Lee eventually announced that the autopsy attributed his death of a rare fatal reaction to two types of prescribed medication he had been taking. Whatever the reason, the loss was a difficult one to accept, and thus paved the way for a variety of cinematic rip-off Bruce Li's and Bruce Le's. If one is looking to discover a "proper" tribute to Lee, it's recommended that they pick up *Kentucky Fried Movie*. Directed by John Landis and written by the *Airplane/Naked Gun* team of Jim Abrahams and David and Jerry Zucker, the film features a spoof of **Enter the Dragon** entitled "A Fistful of Yen." It is a perfect parody/homage to that film and Bruce Lee.

The **Game of Death** was inspired by a trip to India taken

by Lee, actor James Coburn and screenwriter Stirling Silliphant for the proposed **Silent Flute**, which was eventually made with David Carradine and retitled **Circle of Iron**. Lee developed a vague but intriguing concept for a film. In it, he would portray a martial artist—reportedly Tang Lung from **Way (Return) of the Dragon**—in search of a holy relic placed on the top level of a pagoda. Getting there, however, would be no easy task as each level of the pagoda was guarded by a master of a particular martial art, who he would have to defeat.

"No script had yet been worked out," Linda Lee and Tom Bleecker wrote in *The Bruce Lee Story*, "but he had a vague idea which would involve bringing some of the world's greatest martial artists and athletes together. Then he heard that his old friend Kareem Abdul-Jabbar was paying a visit to Hong Kong. Bruce called him and suggested that they do a fight scene together, having envisioned that almost nothing could be more interesting than to see him battling against a man almost two feet taller. Kareem agreed enthusiastically and for a week they planned and then shot

## GAME OF DEATH: TRIBUTE TO A FRIEND, NOW A LEGEND

**Game of Death** is, in the words of its producer Raymond Chow, "a tribute to a friend who became a legend—Bruce Lee."

It took Chow some time before he could get past an admitted "emotional block" about Lee's death. "The Bruce Lee films broke box office records and gave Golden Harvest its entree into the international market," explained Chow. "Lee was our greatest star...and my friend."

The overwhelming success of his films—"Bruce was also a fine actor," says director Robert Clouse—and his enormous following among students and fans of the Oriental art he single-handedly popularized, prompted Chow and Clouse to take another look at the **Game of Death** footage. It was cinematic gold. Lee had fought not only world karate champions Bob Wall, Danny Inosanto and Chuck Norris, but also basketball great, Kareem Abdul-Jabbar.

Screenwriter Jan Spears made intricate modifications to the original **Game of Death** script. Small parts were enlarged, and top talents were brought in to fill what had now become major roles. It was all shot against the exotic Eastern backdrop of Hong Kong and Macao.

At least four local records were broken during the film-making: a stadium to seat 3,000 people was built in 11 days, a 70-foot wall, strong enough to support heavy neon signs, was built in a week, more extras were used than in any other Hong Kong-based movie made, Panavision's Panaglide floating camera mechanism was used for the first time in any feature film shot in Hong Kong.

The special effects team made 3,000 square feet of "breakway" glass so that a three-man American stunt motorcycle team could blast through it in one of the film's more hair-raising sequences.

Many of those working on the film had known Lee personally, so such problems as the heat, the threat of typhoons, water-rationing (use limited to six hours a day—a real headache when scenes called for monsoons) and the language barriers were contended with in relative calm.

In the end, sets and furniture were built in record time by skilled craftsmen, also fans of Lee...and the typhoons decided to spare Hong Kong and concentrate on Taiwan. Bruce Lee's **Game of Death** was

some of the most fantastic and beautiful fight scenes ever filmed."

Lee did go on to shoot fight scenes with a nunchaku-wielding Dan Inosanto (a friend and protege) and hapkido expert Chi Hon Joi. At that point, however, he was inundated with film offers and accepted **Enter the Dragon**. The intention was to go back to **Game of Death** upon completing that film, but this was never to be.

In the wake of Lee's death, everyone was trying desperately to keep the cash register ringing via the aforementioned rip-off films and supposed successors to the Little Dragon. Raymond Chow in particular seemed intent on keeping the phenomenon in motion. One rumored project—and a pointless one at that—was a full length animated Bruce Lee movie. Thankfully this piece of exploitation never moved beyond the talking stage, but what did make it to the screen was nearly as bad. Chow had obtained the footage Lee had shot for **Game of Death**, and announced that there was over a hundred minutes of film. Robert Clouse would be brought in to shoot supposed bridging sequences with doubles for Lee named Jim Tai Chug and Chen Yao Po.

**Game of Death** was heralded by Columbia Pictures as Lee's greatest film and scheduled for release in 1978. As it unspooled, however, audiences were stunned. If there had been over a hundred minutes of footage shot by Lee, it certainly never made it to the screen. Lee is clearly seen in fight scenes but only in those few moments of screen time! His doubles are painfully obvious, reminding one of Bela Lugosi's ludicrous "double" used to finish his scenes in the awful *Plan Nine From Outer Space* following his death. In addition, the storyline of a martial artist nobly attempting to retrieve an artifact of his people was replaced by one in which an actor attempts to fight back against a ruthless agent trying to control his career. This is *not* a

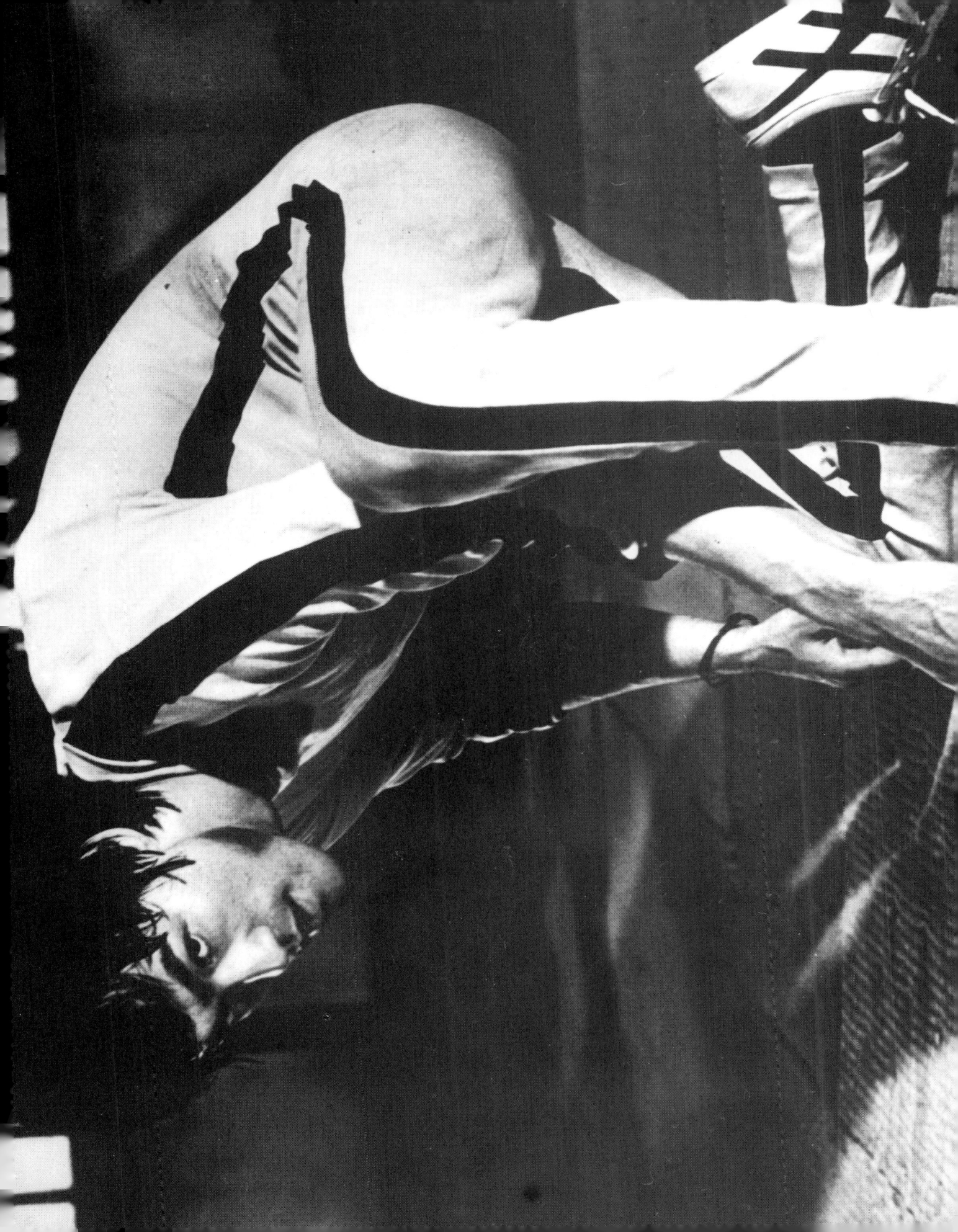

simplification of the plot, it is the entirety of the actual motivation in the film.

Except for the fight sequence with Kareem Abdul-Jabbar, **Game of Death** was an inappropriate conclusion to an incredible film career. It did worse than nothing to enhance the legend of Bruce Lee.

## The Story

The main titles of **Game of Death**, accompanied by a terrific John (007) Barry theme, indicate that the audience is in for one hell of a good time at the movies. The stirring music joins clips from Lee's previous films, all superimposed over the images of games of chance. The whole thing has the feel of a James Bond title sequence, and one could easily believe that it was done by that series' Maurice Binder, although such is not the case.

Unfortunately, the movie itself starts after that. The film opens with the climactic fight from **Return of the Dragon,** but intercut with this is a film crew shooting what is now a sequence in Billy Lo's (Bruce Lee) new kung fu film. Chuck Norris falls before his opponent, a director yells "cut" and a Bruce Lee double walks off-stage, barely avoiding a falling kieg light. A shot of the real Lee looking up is inserted and the camera dwells on the roof of the studio. This would work if the inserted shot didn't very obviously take place outside.

Billy goes into his dressing room. Another insert shot of Lee follows, and then the double is shown talking to Steiner (Hugh O'Brian), who wants to control his acting career. He threatens Billy with physical violence if the isn't cooperative, and then leaves. Before he does, however, the camera shows a horrible image of a Bruce Lee photo headshot with someone else's body standing behind it. Terrible filming! Billy strikes out and is told by Steiner that that was a mistake.

Billy meets his girlfriend Ann Morris (Colleen Camp), who he's picking up for dinner. Meanwhile, Dr. Land (maniacally played by Dean Jagger) meets with Steiner and they discuss their problem. A quote from the pressbook best explains the film at this point: "Kung fu superstar Billy Lo wants to say 'No' to signing a lifetime 'contract' with the Syndicate, an international criminal organization specializing in the exploitation of top talent in films, theatre, music and sports. Ruthless Syndicate czar Doctor Land orders his suave and sinister aide, Steiner, to pressure Billy and his girlfriend into obeying." And that's the initial plot in a nutshell.

Billy, his eyes hidden by sunglasses (any guesses as to why?) and Ann are driving to dinner to discuss the pressures being exerted upon them. Before Billy can respond to her, their car is surrounded by three ominous motorcyclists. Steiner approaches the car and Billy gets out. Steiner says he has until the next day to sign a contract with them. At that moment, a fight beaks out. The choreography is handled reasonable well, but Billy is ultimately overpowered.

Later, at a restaurant, Billy's friend Jim Marshall (Gig Young) suggests that he sign, reminding him of a friend who tried to fight the Syndicate. This is intercut with footage of Kareem Abdul-Jabbar as Hakim, killing a fighter (one assumes this had been shot by Lee). Meanwhile, the Syndicate decides to give Billy a final chance.

The next day, Billy visits his uncle, an actor, and they discuss the Syndicate's desires. His uncle suggests that if Billy wants his independence, he should "push" back. A pair of motorcyclists enter the area and another fight breaks out. This time, Billy is nearly victorious, until Carl Miller

# BRUCE LEE: MARTIAL ARTS SUPERSTAR, FILM PHENOMENON

*(from the promotional material)*

The legend of Bruce Lee, world-famous martial arts master, reaches a new peak this year with the Columbia Pictures release of his last and most action-packed film, **Game of Death**.

Also staring Academy Award-winners Dean Jagger and Gig Young, with basketball great Kareem Abdul-Jabber, Hugh O'd Brian and Colleen Camp, **Game of Death** pits Lee against a criminal syndicate out to exploit stars in the world of films, music, theatre and sports. It is the fifth martial arts film starring Lee.

The first Chinese-American to become a global superstar—who did more to popularize martial arts than anyone before or since—was born in San Francisco in 1940. Originally named Lee Yuen Kam, meaning "Protector of San Francisco," he was called Bruce by a nurse who thought he should have a suitable Western name.

He was raised in Hong Kong, where his father, Lee Ho Chuen, was a Cantonese opera comedy star. Paternal introductions got Lee into Asian films and he appeared in 20 of them during his childhood.

Paternal instructions in "Tai Chi Chaun" exercises led to Lee's consuming interest in martial arts at 13. For two years he studied the Chinese Kung-Fu and Chinese Boxing at the Wing Chuen school under Yip Man.

At 18, with $100 to his name, the intense young Lee returned on a freighter to San Francisco to retain his American citizenship.

Fanatical about Kung Fu, he practiced continually—even on lawns at the University of Washington, where he was a philosophy major. After marrying a fellow student, he moved to Oakland and opened a "Jun Fan" school with James Lee.

To promote it, Bruce Lee toured the Western states and finally, at Long Beach, California, gave a demonstration which caught the eye of a television producer who cast Lee as Kato in television's **The Green Hornet**. The series was short-lived, but Lee's impact remained. He soon made **Marlowe** with James Garner and **Longstreet** with James Franciscus.

Lee's dramatic introduction of Kung Fu, Karate, Judo and other martial arts popularized the sports almost overnight.

He taught the science to many, including such well-known names as Steve McQueen, James Garner, Elke Sommer, David Carradine (star of television's hit series, *Kung Fu*), James Coburn and Kareem Abdul-Jabbar, the basketball great whose karate duel with Lee is one of the highlights of **Game of Death**.

He is said to have passed on his vast store of knowledge to one man only—Danny Inosanto, a world champion also in Lee's final film.

Behind the mystique, however, beat the heart of a film-maker.

Dissatisfied with the way Chinese and the martial arts were portrayed in films at the time, Lee leapt at the chance to do his kind of picture at the invitation of producer Raymond Chow, head of the Hong Kong based entertainment conglomerate, The Golden Harvest Group.

Lee's first picture for Chow, **The Big Boss** (retitled **Fists of Fury** in the U.S.) grossed over $12 million, an Asian box-office record at the time (1972). His next, **Fists of Fury** (**The Chinese Connection** in the U.S.) earned over $15 million. In 1973, his third (sic) **Enter the Dragon**, grossed $100 million world-wide and firmly established young Lee as an international star whose films were almost guaranteed to be successful. For his fourth film (sic), **Way of the Dragon** (retitled **Return of the Dragon** in the U.S.), Lee directed his action scenes for the first time. It was another blockbuster.

He was, however, a young man in a hurry. Without stopping, he plunged right into his fifth and most carefully-wrought film, **Game of Death**. One hundred minutes of the dramatic action—planned, choreographed and shot by Lee—were completed when he died unexpectedly.

Some who knew him feel he simply strained himself past the breaking point. Others speculate other causes. The official verdict was "death by misadventure," leaving an aura of mystery to the legend of Bruce Lee. Whatever the reason, his death was difficult to accept. And his film, showing him at his most polished, most spirited, lay unfinished for five years. Until now. (from the promotional material)

(Bob Wall, who also played Oharra in **Enter the Dragon**) defeats him.

Back at the Syndicate, Steiner realizes that Billy is not going to sign and points out that rebellion is contagious. He insists Billy must be disposed of. Dr. Land agrees, although he thinks it a terrible waste of talent.

Billy calls Ann and asks her to meet him on the six o'clock ferry. She does so and he says she should go back to the United States. He has one more scene to shoot for the film, then he'll disappear. They'll get together in a couple of months, and grow old with each other. Unfortunately, all of this has been overheard by a member of the Syndicate. Later, Ann calls Marshall and says she thinks Billy is going to fight the organization. Marshall says he'll meet with her.

On the movie set, actors for the climactic scene of the kung fu film are armed with blanks, but a Syndicate member loads a very real bullet in his gun. Billy readies his scene, which consists of a run, leap and fall. Marshall and Ann confront him and he admits that he's going to fight the Syndicate. He pleads with Jim to take her to the airport, and then gets back to work.

The camera begins to roll and footage from the climax of **The Chinese Connection** is inserted, making use of the scene in which Bruce Lee makes his final leap to death. For this new film, new footage is similar in that Billy is shot by the Syndicate member. Ann, who has not yet left, and the crew are horrified to discover that Billy has been shot in the face. He lives, but at the hospital we learn that his face has been permanently disfigured (which works out quite conveniently for the film as the audience can no longer expect the character to continue looking exactly like Bruce Lee). Jim Marshall and the hospital chief along with Billy concoct a tale for the press that Billy Lo is dead.

His fans are devastated by the news, very much mirroring the reaction to Bruce Lee's real death. A funeral is held, intercut with footage of Billy undergoing plastic surgery. This moment works rather well, and achieves strong emotional impact.

Ann leaves the funeral in tears and eventually suffers something of a nervous breakdown. Marshall visits her at the sanitarium. He suggests she go back to the States, but she's not ready to do so. Meanwhile, Steiner and Dr. Land, in a limousine, discuss the possibility that Ann might be a threat to them. Soon thereafter, following Marshall's departure, they arrive at the sanitarium and try to get her to let them help, but she accuses them of being murderers. Dr. Land gets back in his limo, angry that she was such a "rude bitch."

Billy gets out of the hospital, not looking much different than the "double" shown all along. Only this time he has a moustache and beard. He follows Syndicate members to a dock, where he sees them board a hydrofoil. He hires a boat to follow them.

Ann calls Marshall, telling him that she knows who killed Billy. He tells her to meet him.

Billy asks the captain of his boat to wait for him and pursues Dr. Land and the others to a limo. He gets in a cab and begins to follow. They go to Syndicate headquarters, where they meet some people sponsoring a major karate tournament. Billy gets on the property and moves swiftly. Soon he stands before Dr. Land, who he starts to strangle. Guards show up and Billy, apparently tired of being knocked out, beats them, the actor thankfully looking better in the fight scene than he did earlier.

Dr. Land makes a run for it. Miller fights Billy, and he holds his own until Steiner starts shooting. Then Billy takes off. Soon, Dr. Land, Steiner and the others realize that the intruder not only wanted to kill Land, but wanted to punish him as well. Also, there was something familiar about the man, but they can't place it.

At the karate tournament, Miller fights his opponent. Ann nears the doctor in the stands, withdrawing a gun from her purse. An old man (actually Billy in disguise) tells her to let it go, "that what needs to be done is being done." Miller is ultimately victorious in the battle. Going into the locker room, he is confronted by the old man, who reveals himself to be Billy. Head-shots of Bruce Lee are inserted, which casts a question on the rationale behind the plastic surgery being performed as an excuse for the change in features. Billy looks exactly the way he did at he outset. Perhaps this was just a way to fill screen time. The two men begin fighting, and the Lee double is again painfully obvious. A series of powerful (though a bit sloppily choreographed) kicks take care of Miller, resulting in the man's death. Dr. Land is *not* a happy maniac.

The mad doctor tells Steiner to dig up Billy's body to make sure he's really buried. Elsewhere, Billy is talking to Jim, trying to arrange a time he can meet Ann. Unfortunately the line is tapped.

At the cemetery, Steiner discovers that Billy's body is merely a mannequin.

Ann and Billy meet. His dialogue implies that he's not ready to face her until he faces himself, apparently discussing the plastic surgery. The whole concept grows more preposterous by the second! Billy once again asks her to go to the States. She departs, but is eventually kidnapped by syndicate motorcyclists, so that she can be used as "bait".

Later, Steiner meets Marshall and tells him to have Billy meet the Syndicate at a local warehouse at 1AM. If he comes alone, Ann will be set free. Jim goes to his office.

Billy's on the phone. He conveys the message and Billy agrees to meet them.

Arriving at the warehouse, Billy finds a bound Ann. He sets upon freeing her, when the motorcyclists in waiting try to smash their way in. Another shot of Bruce Lee's face is inserted. The motorcyclists smash through windows and move in for the kill. Billy knocks out a yellow-clad driver and puts on his outfit, which just happens to match the jumpsuit worn by Lee in his original **Game of Death** footage. Billy disposes of the drivers one-by-one, with some fairly well executed stunts involving the motorcycles. Billy beats one of the men until he reveals that Dr. land is at the Red Pepper restaurant. As the climax approaches, the frustration mounts if you know Lee's original vision of this story. His intriguing concept of a pagoda is transformed into an ordinary Chinese restaurant.

Billy sets off (presumably freeing Ann in the process), while Land is panicking because he's unable to reach anyone at the warehouse. We see a ridiculous looking supposed double for Lee enter the restaurant and climb the steps to the next level, while picking up a couple of weapons from a wall display.

At this moment, **Game of Death** footage is utilized, as it is the real Bruce Lee we see reach the second level. In other words, a double sets foot on the staircase, and the real Bruce Lee arrives at the top. There he confronts Pasqual (Dan Inosanto), who utilizes stick weapons. Billy disarms him of one, and the man casts off the other, to take a pair of nunchukas. Billy pulls out his own. The two men begin to battle, the blurring nunchukas whipping all across the camera frame. They strike each other viciously, but Billy eliminates his opponent with a series of kicks and then by wrapping the nunchuka around the man's throat and breaking his neck.

Billy (actually, for the moment, let's refer to him as Lee to distinguish this sequence from other parts of the bizarre film) proceeds to the next level (this is some strange restaurant, huh?), where he comes up against a hapkido expert, and a terrific fight unfolds, accompanied by John Barry's wonderful music. The fight is wonderful film, with both Lee and his opponent moving like magic. The sequence culminates with Lee breaking the man's back.

Lee is weary from what he's suffered through, but a creaking sound from above forces him to compose himself as he ascends to the third level. His reaction to his opponent's height is quite funny, as he stares up at Hakim (Kareem Abdul-Jabbar). Hakim just takes a seat, and as Lee approaches, he kicks out, sending Lee reeling backwards. As the fight intensifies, it's amazing to witness the difference in size between these two warriors. Lee gets in a few good shots, and then cockily motions for Hakim to join him in the center of the room. The man agrees and the conflict continues. Utilizing his incredible speed, Lee dazes the giant and slowly but surely "chops" him down with a series of powerful punches and kicks. Finally, Lee wraps his arms around the man's neck and drags him across the floor. Hakim tries to stand and shake him off, but Lee breaks his neck.

The imagery of the last fight and the incredible choreography on Lee's part, *almost* saves this film, but not quite. These two opponents going after each other has to be seen to be believed.

The film returns to its usual mediocre level as Steiner calls out to Hakim and comes down the stairs wielding his bladed cane. Billy (the double is back) trips him. A fight breaks out between the two, with occasional shots of Bruce Lee horribly edited in. The most ludicrous part of this whole fight is the incredible length of time it takes to conclude, particularly after the battle with Hakim. There is simply no way Steiner could give Billy this much trouble. The sequence ends with the man being kicked down a flight of stairs to his death.

Billy then climbs to the top level of the restaurant, where he is stunned to find (and inserts of Lee are put to good effect here) Dr. Land at his desk, apparently dead as his wrists have been slit. This, however, ridiculously turns out to be a wax dummy, which leaves the viewer wondering why the villains would go through so much trouble, and when they found the time to do so in the first place. Billy pursues the real Land to the roof of the building, and in an attempt to escape, plunges to his death.

The credits roll, as a James Bond-type theme song plays and more clips from past Lee films fill the screen.

What can be said? **Game of Death** is a pretty terrible film. Why Columbia Pictures wasn't taken to court for false advertising is the only real remaining question. *One hundred minutes of footage shot by Lee* ? Where?! To be fair, the brief amount of footage shown with Lee is tremendous, and one has to give director Robert Clouse credit for a valiant effort trying to make the whole stupid thing work. The stunts and fight scenes are acceptable, being helped immeasurably by the John Barry score. But the odds were against this project from the beginning.

The bottom line is that what was supposed to have been a tribute to the memory of Bruce Lee, was delivered as another in a long line of rip-offs.

## PRODUCTION NOTES

*(from the promotional material)*

Bruce Lee, the legendary martial arts hero, stars as a movie idol who fights to keep his career from being taken over by the underworld in **Game of Death**.

The Columbia Pictures release was the final movie Lee made, prior to his untimely—and to some, mysterious—death at the age of 32. More than 100 minutes of action, including a climactic Karate battle with 7'2" basketball great, Kareem Abdul-Jabbar, had been filmed and are integrated into the exotic thriller, set in Hong Kong.

A Golden Harvest Film, the Raymond Chow production is the fifth showcase for Lee's deft maneuvers in such arts as Karate, Kung Fu and the split-second use of the deadly Nanchukas sticks.

Lee's four previous films—**Fists of Fury, The Chinese Connection, Return of the Dragon** and **Enter the Dragon**—made the Kung Fu champion the first Chinese-American superstar around the world, and kicked off the enormous popularity of martial arts in this country. All four were produced by his friend Raymond Chow and directed by Robert Clouse [sic], who perform the same duties for **Game of Death**.

Written by Jan Spears, **Game of Death** co-stars Academy Award-winner Gig Young as a Hong Kong-based newsman who befriends Lee in his fight against Syndicate czar Dean Jagger, also an Oscar-winner. Colleen Camp, of television's *Rich Man, Poor Man*, plays Lee's singer-girlfriend, and Hugh O'Brian (of *Wyatt Earp* fame) portrays Jagger's suave and sinister aide.

Shot on location in Hong Kong and Macao, **Game of Death** features Mel Novak, Roy Chaio and martial arts stars Bob Wall, Danny Inosanto and Chuck Norris. The "electrically charged film," to quote director Clouse, "contains the most spectacular footage the Chinese-American superstar ever filmed. It is, we feel, a fitting memorial to Bruce Lee." (from the promotional material)

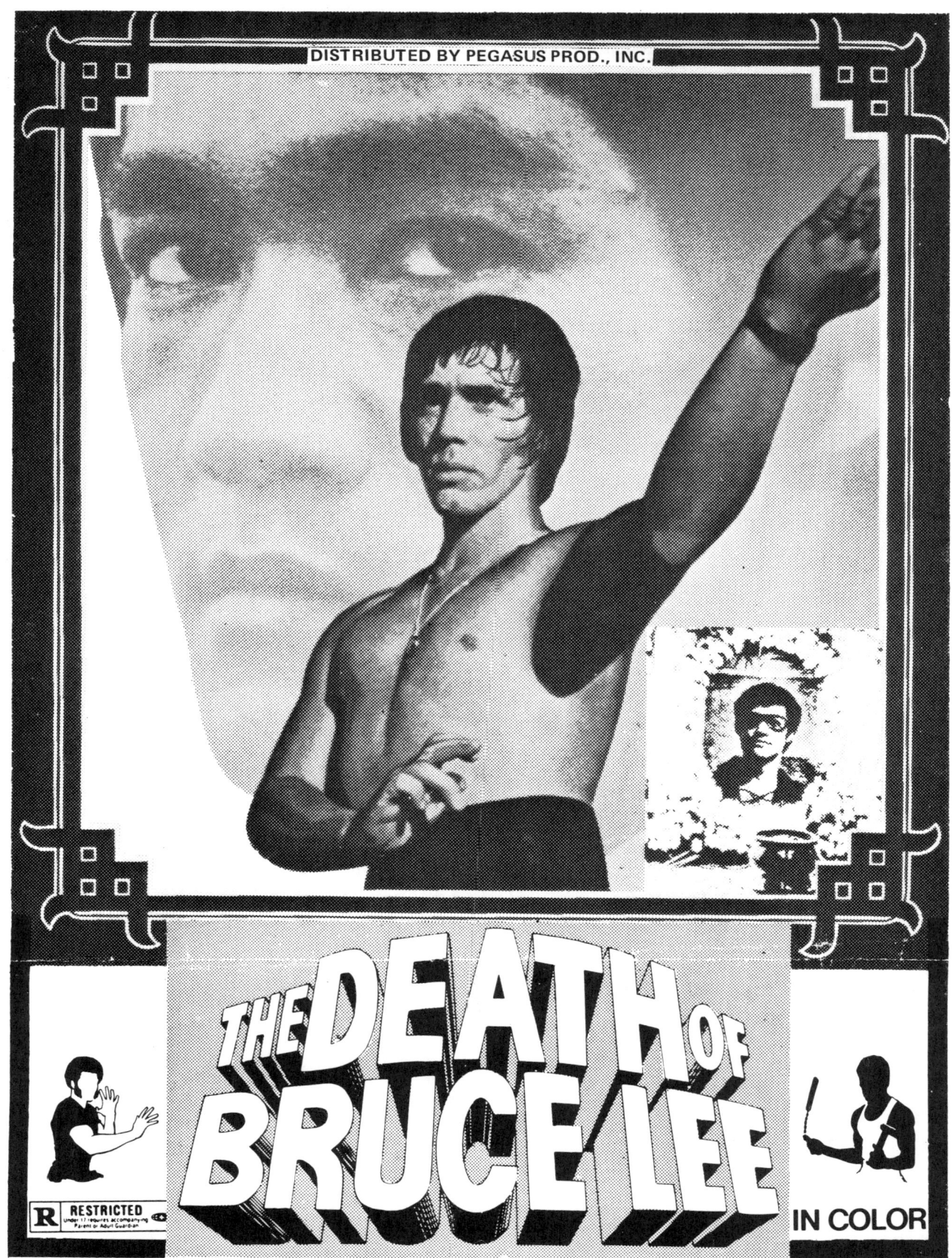

# Conclusion

Through the course of his four motion pictures and the footage he shot for **Game of Death**, Bruce Lee achieved incredible growth as an actor and film-maker. He passed from beginning his adult film career in a genre that had ended the livelihood of so many others to finding the world within his easy reach.

Lee recognized the limitations of the kung fu genre and grew determined to elevate himself beyond them. He knew that America was the key. If he could make it there, then he could make it anywhere, and the reaction to **Enter the Dragon** proved that he had.

That film gave audiences indication of where he would be going as an actor. And they accepted it enthusiastically.

Naturally this is only conjecture, but one could see Lee transforming one of his characters into an Oriental James Bond involved with colorful villains hellbent on world domination. His opponents became larger-than-life, just as they in the Bond films. Lee was ready to take this major step and emerge from the realm of typical martial arts films just as death claimed him.

For further proof, observe his footage in **Game of Death** where he pits himself against Kareem Abdul-Jabbar's Hakim, clearly a Bond-type henchman.

In addition, there would eventually have been less of an emphasis on fight scenes—a cutting back, not a removal of this vital energetic element of storytelling—and more attention devoted to story and character. This step would have guaranteed Lee greater longevity in Hollywood. Other action stars had made this step prior to Lee, such as John Wayne. Others have followed, including Chuck Norris, who has already made nearly 20 films. It also seems to be working for the newest genre hero, Steven Seagal.

Despite the fact that Bruce Lee was taken from us at the painfully young age of 32, he has achieved an immortality

in the hearts and minds of his fans. People not born until *after* his death have discovered his work and taken his philosophy to heart, passing the legend of Bruce Lee down to their children in turn.

The Little Dragon is dead. Long live the Little Dragon.

Long live Bruce Lee!

# APPENDIX
## The Silent Flute
## a.k.a. Circle Of Iron

Any artist must possess the ability to dream, and Bruce Lee was no exception. All his life he had dreamt of achieving stardom in the martial arts world and as an actor, and it was a goal he—quite obviously—had finally obtained.

"The first time I saw him," said actor James Coburn in *Black Belt's Bruce Lee Memorial Book*, "I had no doubt that he was the greatest martial artist that I had ever witnessed; probably one of the greatest of all time. And he knew it, too. It wasn't a question of him competing with anybody. It was a question of everybody else competing with him, because he was like the beacon, the source of the energy that everybody got something from.

"[Success] was something that he had always wanted more than anything else: the success of achieving something with martial arts without making any compromises anywhere down the line—absolutely none."

The vehicle that Lee had believed would transport him down the road of success was **The Silent Flute**, a concept he had developed with students and friends James Coburn and writer Stirling Silliphant.

Linda Lee and Tom Bleecker in *The Bruce Lee Story* wrote, "**The Silent Flute** contained many of the themes that reflected Bruce's life and behavior. The script traced a young student's evolution through the martial arts—his problem of ego, his newfound courage in facing the abyss of death and finally his spiritual rebirth. At one point in the script, Bruce says, 'I'm not even sure what trials I passed through or how I came to be here. I still have doubts, many doubts. How, without more struggle, can I resolve them?'"

When the screenplay was finished in 1969, the trio handed it to Warner Brothers, who reacted favorably. They were willing to finance the film on a modest budget, provided it be shot in India. The company owned a considerable

amount of money in that country which India refused to release to the United States.

Lee and Bleeker added, "Although India was nobody's idea of the right locale for a Chinese story, the three men intrepidly set off, hoping for the best. Jim Coburn was to be the 'name' in the film, but Bruce, who was to play five different roles, would unquestionably dominate the story. Altogether they spent three weeks in India, trying to find the right place. The idea of course was that if satisfactory locales could be found, some of the Indian martial artists would be used in the film, and thus reduce the below-the-line budget considerably."

Unfortunately, Bruce Lee felt that it would take a minimum of three years to train them properly. Dejected, they left the country and dropped the project, each going on to their respective careers. Several years passed, with Coburn and Silliphant coming back to Lee about the project, but by that time he had achieved a great deal of international success, and perhaps felt he had moved beyond the material. After Lee's death, Coburn and Silliphant tried to revive it once again.

"Twentieth Century Fox has it currently," Coburn said at the time, "and we hope to start shooting this spring in Japan, Turkey and Iran, if we can find somebody to play Bruce's part. We have altered it to make it more of a philosophical concept than a physical one, using the physical fights as the motor and moving toward more of an esoteric bent than a physical one. That's what it's about—higher principles. That's why we wrote it. It's a great screenplay. With Bruce in it, it would have been marvelous."

Several years later, **The Silent Flute** made it to the screen under the title **Circle of Iron**. It strarred David Carradine in the roles designated for Lee, with newcomer Jeff Cooper in the Coburn role of Corg.

The authors of *The Bruce Lee Story* didn't view the film favorably. "Years after Bruce's death **The Silent Flute** was made into a film," they wrote, "or should I say a film was made that had some semblance to the original script. Screen credit was given to Bruce in the form of 'Story Originated by Bruce Lee' [Coburn and Silliphant also received credit]. Perhaps the producers thought that adding Bruce's name to the credits would embellish the movie's appeal. I'm sure Bruce would have wished they had not bothered, since the final product was far removed from anything he had envisioned."

While far from a martial arts masterpiece, **Circle of Iron** is not a bad film. Taking place in ancient times, it begins with Corg seeking the book of ultimate knowledge, the one that unlocks the secrets of the universe. During the course of his quest, he encounters the blind prophet who can teach him about himself while leading him in the right direction. On and off, the blind man vanishes and in his place appears a tribe of men dressed as apes, a black panther-like vision of death and Chongsha (all played by Carradine), an enigmatic prince whose path Corg crosses twice. Each of these provide another clue as to Corg's path to self-discovery, culminating in his obtaining the book of knowledge from a group of individuals (led by Christopher Lee) who have been guarding it, awaiting the arrival of the newest seekers. Corg is urged not to look at its pages, but after all he's been through, he must.

Slowly he opens the book and is stunned to find that each page is a mirror. As he stares upon his reflection, all the universe is revealed to him.

**Circle of Iron** moves slowly in spots, but is beautifully photographed. The fight sequences work fairly well, and while Jeff Cooper has some problems in his role, David Carradine does a nice turn in his various personas. Carradine can indeed appear wooden on film, but here he successfully creates distinct characterizations.

Watching this film, however, one can't help but wonder what it would have been like had Bruce Lee lived to play the leading roles.

Co-founder of Panavision, turned cinematographer, turned director, Richard Moore explains **Circle of Iron**, "It's a goofy little film that sort of fell between the cracks. For kung fu aficionados it was far too esoteric, and for the mainstream audience it was too much chop-sockey. It didn't do too much business, I'm certain of that. I had a great deal of fun working on it.

"I was actually aware of the film long before I became involved with it. I had owned an office building, and one of my offices was rented by Bruce Lee, Stirling Silliphant and James Coburn. I knew they were working on something. I had no idea at the time what is was they were doing. After Lee died, the project apparently went into hiatus for some time, and then Sandy Howard got a hold of it and added two plus two, putting David Carradine—who was hot off of *Kung Fu*—into the role that Lee was to play. It made sense, and from that standpoint it had a certain amount of appeal to it.

"The difficulty, and I don't like to bad mouth anything but we have to deal with reality, and the one big negative aspect of making the film, was the casting of Corg, who's on camera all the time. Carradine insisted on using his old martial arts buddy, Jeff Cooper. Jeff is a sweet, sweet guy, but he couldn't act his way out of a paper bag. It was very difficult in the sense that I had a choice of trying to get a performance out of him and going way over budget and over schedule, or hoping for the best and staying with the budget and schedule, and let the chips fall where they may. I decided that this was my first directorial job, and I didn't think I'd ever get what we needed from Cooper, so we might as well go for the other alternative, which was to bring it in on budget and on schedule. In my humble opinion, his performance is awfully hard to swallow for me and I think for a lot of other people too.

"What Sandy bought from the guys who owned it was thirty pages of the most incredibly esoteric, non-cinematic stuff I've ever read. I don't know how the hell they would have ever expected to make it into a film. What Sandy did was to bring in Stanley Mann, who fleshed it out into a 120 page script. What we ended up with was a far cry from what they had conceived. They were going to do the definitive Zen martial arts film, as I recall. You would have had 30 people look at it.

"I personally think that Carradine did something kind of unique there, and I think he pulled it off. He plays four different parts. He plays the blind man, the monkey man, Chongsha and he also played the part of the panther man. His characterizations from one to the other, for him, were pretty good. I thought he'd done a minor tour de force there. A lot of actors couldn't do that.

"The thing that attracted me so much to the script was the ending wherein all of life's secrets in the great book are nothing but mirrors. I loved that, a lot. The film says that knowledge of all of life's problems and opportunities are not to be found in any book. The answers to all of your questions in life must be found in yourself. I really think that's true. In today's world which is becoming increasingly complex, people search for solutions in someone else's writings or speeches, and eventually you have to make your own decisions and they can only be made from within yourself."

# Successors to the throne?

The demise of Bruce Lee caused a traumatic reaction on the part of his fans as well as on the kung fu/martial arts genre. Ironically, his death almost ended the art form he virtually single-handedly launched.

Even beyond the myriad Bruce Li, Bruce Le and Lee Bruce clones, others attempted to grasp the Little Dragon's mantle, but failed. The box office impact of **Enter the Dragon** led America into the sweepstakes, with only moderate success until the arrival of Chuck Norris.

Karate champion Chuck Norris appeared with Bruce Lee in **Return of the Dragon**'s climactic battle in the Roman Coliseum. Several years later, he starred in such films as *Good Guys Wear Black, A Force of One, Silent Rage* and *Missing in Action*. The last turned out to be the most successful independent film of 1984, and the first to deal with the concept of a Vietnam vet retrieving POWs. Norris touched a chord in the public conscience, and in 1985 earned the respect of critics as well with *Code of Silence*.

Norris' critical acceptance was a long time in coming, as reviewers and the public alike gradually discovered that his films offered more than standard kung fu fare. Like Bruce Lee, Chuck Norris surmounted the limitations of the genre to deliver something finer.

"If you look at my movies," he explains, "none of them were intertwined with karate. I never really did what you would consider a karate movie. In one, I was a professional kick boxer, but it wasn't a kung fu type of movie. It dealt with a professional fighter, like Rocky. In *Good Guys Wear Black*, I was a college professor who got involved in all this political intrigue, and who just happened to know how to use karate. I had done a movie with Bruce Lee, **Return of the Dragon**, and because it was a kung fu movie, I got labeled from the first film and people called me a karate actor. It was really a hard nut to crack all these years—to try to tell them that I'm *not* doing a kung fu or karate movie. A kung fu movie is when you open with a fight scene and fight all the way through the film for no rhyme or reason. I never wanted to do a movie like that—one which had no emotional contact. So I did use karate in my movies, but in situations where it was *emotionally* involved. When I got into a fight in one of those films, I couldn't fight like John Wayne used to in the '50s, which would have been outdated. So I went with a modern method of fighting in the 80s, the martial arts type of fighting. People in the media immediately said, 'Kung fu artist Chuck Norris does so-and-so movie...'

"Probably the toughest part," Norris adds, "is handling the criticism. In every movie, I put my whole heart and soul into it, and negative criticisms really hurt. You have to have a tough crust in this business. I jumped right into film and so I got hit pretty hard in the beginning. But it has lightened up from movie to movie, and *Code of Silence* really opened up the door for me to acceptance.

"I don't know what led me to film. I think I'm a goal seeker. I had become complacent with the martial arts field; I had accomplished basically what I wanted to in that world. I needed a new challenge to respark my vitality. Steve McQueen is the one who really got me into it, because I hadn't really considered acting. McQueen brought it up, telling me that I would be good, though no one could know for sure, but it was worth going for. I thought about it for four or five months before I made the choice. Once I make up my mind, I go for it. I sold my karate schools and gave up all my businesses."

As noted, his first attempt at acting came in Bruce Lee's **Return of the Dragon**.

"Bruce Lee was a good friend," he recalls warmly, "and he said, 'I want to do a movie with a big fight scene that everybody will remember. I want you to be my opponent.' I said yes and we went to Rome to shoot the big battle in the Coliseum. *That* was my total involvement. Of course, that fight scene has now become a classic."

Norris admits that he was a little surprised by the sudden critical acclaim in 1985. "Truthfully, I don't know what was different about *Code of Honor*. I still used karate in it. I guess there has been a slow transition for

## SPECIAL SECTION

them to really accept me, mainly because of my inadequacy in the earlier days. I jumped into films without any real training, so it took me nine years to grow into an acceptable actor. The problem is that the critics were trying to put me in the Dustin Hoffman category. I'm *not* a Dustin Hoffman. I have no desire to be an actor's actor; a guy who plays from one extreme to another. I've developed a certain character that I enjoy doing and as long as the audience likes the character, I'll do it. They're the ones who decide. I have become a personality, just like Clint Eastwood, Sylvester Stallone and Charles Bronson. You just have to accept it; that's how your destiny is set for you. Whether you can break that and *become* a Dustin Hoffman is another story.

"The bottom line," he adds, "is whether or not people will accept [the films]. Will I be number one with them again? That makes me more nervous than the reviews, because if my movie bombs at the box office, it doesn't get me work. It's nice to have the icing on the cake, which is a good review, but whether or not it's a good movie is more important. *That's* what it's all about."

Since the release of *Code of Silence*, Norris has done a variety of films, including *Invasion USA, Delta Force, Firewalker,* a pair of *Missing in Action* sequels and *The Hero and the Terror,* but the criticisms have started again and the box office takes of each have diminished. His next film is the problem-plagued *Delta Force II*, and its fate is yet to be determined. It seems that America's brief love affair with Chuck Norris has come to a close, and the search for a Bruce Lee successor has begun anew.

One potential candidate is world kickboxing champion Jean Claude Van Damme, who has acted in a variety of motion pictures, including *Black Eagle, Bloodsport, Cyborg, Kickboxer* and *Bloodfist*. While the fight sequences in these efforts have been well choreographed, and Van Damme exerts his best efforts to acting, the critics and public have pretty much ignored his work.

Perhaps the newest successor to the throne is *aikido* expert Steven Seagal who has also turned to acting in *Above the Law* and *Hard to Kill,* a pair of action films that delve into Eastern mysticism and which seem to be establishing him as moviedom's latest action hero.

Seagal himself, ironically, is only moderately pleased with his film career thus far, as he noted in the April, 1990 edition of *Black Belt* magazine.

"I know a lot more about action than anybody else in the business," he stated confidently, "how to cut it, how to choreograph it and even how to shoot it. In *Above the Law* I did not get to do nearly as much as I wanted, didn't have nearly as much control as I wanted, but at least [director] Andy Davis would listen to me most of the time. And at least I was involved in the cutting all of the time. Sometimes he would listen and sometimes he wouldn't. I think the action would have been infinitely better if I could have done it my way. But on *Hard to Kill* I was given a director I don't even think is a director. I think it's a miracle that this guy can put one foot in front of the other. It was a very, very difficult situation. I've never seen anybody in my life who was as much his own worst enemy as this guy. Despite him, I'm hoping we were able to come up with some good stuff.

"My next film, *In a Safe Place*, is my picture; I own it with three other people. I am in charge of all the action in the picture, from every gunshot to every punch and kick. You're going to see fantastic action because there's nobody telling me what to do."

In that same interview, Seagal expressed his respect for Bruce Lee, feeling that there was a striking similarity between them in terms of personal discipline.

"I think Bruce Lee was great," he said. "I think he was a great fighter and a great martial artist. I loved his attitude. I had the fortune to meet him through James Coburn. He was very good. I admired his attitude more than anything. In fact, his attitude reminds me of my attitude in ways, in terms of really wanting to accomplish something and trying hard to get that."

Whether Steven Seagal, or for that matter Chuck Norris and Jean Claude Van Damme, will enjoy longevity in Hollywood remains to be seen. One thing is certain: the search for a new Bruce Lee continues.

THE COUCH POTATO BOOK CATALOG  5715 N BALSAM, LAS VEGAS, NV  89130

# TREK YEAR 1
The earliest voyages and the creation of the series. An in-depth episode guide, a look at the pilots, interviews, character profiles and more... 160 pages...$10.95

# TREK YEAR 2
# TREK YEAR 3
$12.95 each

# THE ANIMATED TREK
Complete in one volume $14.95

# THE MOVIES
The chronicle of all the movies... 116 pages...$12.95

# THE LOST YEARS
For the first time anywhere, the exclusive story of the Star Trek series that almost was including a look at every proposed adventure and an interview with the man that would have replaced Spock. Based on interviews and exclusive research... 160 pages...$14.95

# NEXT GENERATION
Complete background of the new series. Complete first season including character profiles and actor biographies...160 pages ...$19.95

# THE TREK ENCYCLOPEDIA
The reference work to Star Trek including complete information on every character, alien race and monster that ever appeared as well as full information on every single person that ever worked on the series from the stars to the stunt doubles from extras to producers, directors, make-up men and cameramen...**over 360 pages. UPDATED EDITION. Now includes planets, ships and devices**...$19.95

# INTERVIEWS ABOARD THE ENTERPRISE
Interviews with the cast and crew of Star Trek and the Next Generation. From Eddie Murphy to Leonard Nimoy and from Jonathan Frakes to Marina Sirtis. Over 100 pages of your favorites. $18.95

# THE ULTIMATE TREK
The most spectacular book we have ever offered. This volume completely covers every year of Star Trek, every animated episode and every single movie. Plus biographies, interviews, profiles, and more. Over 560 pages! Hardcover only. Only a few of these left. $75.00

# TREK HANDBOOK and TREK UNIVERSE
The Handbook offers a complete guide to conventions, clubs, fanzines.
The Universe presents a complete guide to every book, comic, record and everything else.
Both volumes are edited by Enterprise Incidents editor James Van Hise. Join a universe of Trek fun!
Handbook...$12.95     Universe...$17.95

# THE CREW BOOK
The crew of the Enterprise including coverage of Kirk, Spock, McCoy, Scotty, Uhura, Chekov, Sulu and all the others...plus starship staffing practices...250 pages...$17.95

# THE MAKING OF THE NEXT GENERATION: SCRIPT TO SCREEN
THIS BOOK WILL NOT BE PRINTED UNTIL APRIL OR MAY. Analysis of every episode in each stage, from initial draft to final filmed script. Includes interviews with the writers and directors. 240 pages...$14.95

THE COUCH POTATO BOOK CATALOG  5715 N BALSAM, LAS VEGAS, NV  89130

THE COUCH POTATO BOOK CATALOG 5715 N BALSAM, LAS VEGAS, NV 89130

## THE FREDDY KRUEGER STORY
The making of the monster. Including interviews with director Wes Craven and star Robert Englund. Plus an interview with Freddy himself! $14.95

## THE ALIENS STORY
Interviews with movie director James Cameron, stars Sigourney Weaver and Michael Biehn and effects people and designers Ron Cobb, Syd Mead, Doug Beswick and lots more!...$14.95

## ROBOCOP
Law enforcement in the future. Includes interviews with the stars, the director, the writer, the special effects people, the storyboard artists and the makeup men! $16.95

## MONSTERLAND'S HORROR IN THE '80s
The definitive book of the horror films of the '80s. Includes interviews with the stars and makers of Aliens, Freddy Krueger, Robocop, Predator, Fright Night, Terminator and all the others! $17.95

### LOST IN SPACE

**THE COMPLEAT LOST IN SPACE** 244 PAGES...$17.95

**TRIBUTE BOOK** Interviews with everyone!...$7.95

**TECH MANUAL** Technical diagrams to all of the special ships and devices plus exclusive production artwork....$9.95

### GERRY ANDERSON

**SUPERMARIONATION** Episode guides and character profiles to Capt Scarlet, Stingray, Fireball, Thunderbirds, Supercar and more...240 pages...$17.95

### BEAUTY AND THE BEAST

**THE UNOFFICIAL BEAUTY & BEAST** Complete first season guide including interviews and biographies of the stars. 132 pages $14.95

### DARK SHADOWS

**DARK SHADOWS TRIBUTE BOOK** Interviews, scripts and more... 160 pages...$14.95

**DARK SHADOWS INTERVIEWS BOOK** A special book interviewing the entire cast. $18.95

## DOCTOR WHO THE BAKER YEARS
A complete guide to Tom Baker's seasons as the Doctor including an in-depth episode guide, interviews with the companions and profiles of the characters... 300 pages...$19.95

## THE DOCTOR WHO ENCYCLOPEDIA: THE FOURTH DOCTOR
Encyclopedia of every character, villain and monster of the Baker Years. ..240 pages...$19.95

THE COUCH POTATO BOOK CATALOG  5715 N BALSAM, LAS VEGAS, NV  89130

The Phantom
The Green Hornet
The Shadow
The Batman

Each issue of Serials Adventures Presents offers 100 or more pages of pure nostalgic fun for $16.95

Flash Gordon Part One
Flash Gordon Part Two
Blackhawk

Each issue of Serials Adventures Presents features a chapter by chapter review of a rare serial combined with biographies of the stars and behind-the-scenes information. Plus rare photos. See the videotapes and read the books!

### THE U.N.C.L.E. TECHNICAL MANUAL
Every technical device completely detailed and blueprinted, including weapons, communications, weaponry, organization, facitilites... 80 pages. 2 volumes...$9.95 each

### NUMBER SIX: THE COMPLEAT PRISONER
The most unique and intelligent television series ever aired! Patrick McGoohan's tour-de-force of spies and mental mazes finally explained episode by episode, including an interview with the McGoohan and the complete layout of the real village!...160 pages...$14.95

### THE GREEN HORNET
Daring action adventure with the Green Hornet and Kato. This show appeared before Bruce Lee had achieved popularity but delivered fun, superheroic action. Episode guide and character profiles combine to tell the whole story...120 pages...$14.95

### WILD, WILD, WEST
Is it a Western or a Spy show? We couldn't decide so we're listing it twice. Fantastic adventure, convoluted plots, incredible devices...all set in the wild, wild west! Details of fantastic devices, character profiles and an episode-by-episode guide...120 pages...$17.95

THE COUCH POTATO BOOK CATALOG 5715 N BALSAM, LAS VEGAS, NV  89130

THE COUCH POTATO BOOK CATALOG 5715 N BALSAM, LAS VEGAS, NV 89130

### THE ILLUSTRATED STEPHEN KING

A complee guide to the novels and short stories of Stephen King illustrated by Steve Bissette and others...$12.95

### GUNSMOKE YEARS

The definitive book of America's most successful television series. 22 years of episode guide, character profiles, interviews and more...240 pages, $14.95

### THE KING COMIC HEROES

The complete story of the King Features heroes including Prince Valiant, Flash Gordon, Mandrake, The Phantom, Secret Agent, Rip Kirby, Buz Sawyer, Johnny Hazard and Jungle Jim. These fabulous heroes not only appeared in comic strips and comic books but also in movies and serials. Includes interviews with Hal Foster, Al Williamson and Lee Falk...$14.95

Special discounts are available for library, school, club or other bulk orders. Please inquire.

## IF YOUR FAVORITE TELEVISION SERIES ISN'T HERE, LET US KNOW... AND THEN STAY TUNED!

And always remember that if every world leader was a couch potato and watched TV 25 hours a day, 8 days a week, there would be no war...

THE COUCH POTATO BOOK CATALOG 5715 N BALSAM, LAS VEGAS, NV 89130

**Boring, but Necessary Ordering Information!**

**Payment:** All orders must be prepaid by check or money order. Do not send cash. All payments must be made in US funds only.

**Shipping:** We offer several methods of shipment for our product.

Postage is as follows:

For books priced under $10.00— for the first book add $2.50. For each additional book under $10.00 add $1.00. (This is per individual book priced under $10.00, not the order total.)

For books priced over $10.00— for the first book add $3.25. For each additional book over $10.00 add $2.00. (This is per individual book priced over $10.00, not the order total.)

These orders are filled as quickly as possible. Sometimes a book can be delayed if we are temporarily out of stock. You should note on your order whether you prefer us to ship the book as soon as available or send you a merchandise credit good for other TV goodies or send you your money back immediately. Shipments normally take 2 or 3 weeks, but allow up to 12 weeks for delivery.

**Special UPS 2 Day Blue Label RUSH SERVICE:** Special service is available for desperate Couch Potatos. These books are shipped within 24 hours of when we receive your order and should take 2 days to get from us to you.

For the first **RUSH SERVICE** book under $10.00 add $4.00. For each additional 1 book under $10.00 and $1.25. (This is per individual book priced under $10.00, not the order total.)

For the first **RUSH SERVICE** book over $10.00 add $6.00. For each additional book over $10.00 add $3.50 per book. (This is per individual book priced over $10.00, not the order total.)

**Canadian and Foreign shipping rates are the same** except that Blue Label RUSH SERVICE is not available. All Canadian and Foreign orders are shipped as books or printed matter.

**DISCOUNTS! DISCOUNTS!** Because your orders are what keep us in business we offer a discount to people that buy a lot of our books as our way of saying thanks. On orders over $25.00 we give a 5% discount. On orders over $50.00 we give a 10% discount. On orders over $100.00 we give a 15% discount. On orders over $150.00 we give a 20% discount. Please list alternates when possible. Please state if you wish a refund or for us to backorder an item if it is not in stock.

**100% satisfaction guaranteed.** We value your support. You will receive a full refund as long as the copy of the book you are not happy with is received back by us in reasonable condition. No questions asked, except we would like to know how we failed you. Refunds and credits are given as soon as we receive back the item you do not want.

Please have mercy on Phyllis and carefully fill out this form in the neatest way you can. Remember, she has to read a lot of them every day and she wants to get it right and keep you happy! You may use a duplicate of this order blank as long as it is clear. Please don't forget to include payment! And remember, we *love* repeat friends...

## ORDER FORM

\_\_\_\_\_ The Phantom $16.95
\_\_\_\_\_ The Green Hornet $16.95
\_\_\_\_\_ The Shadow $16.95
\_\_\_\_\_ Flash Gordon Part One $16.95 \_\_\_\_\_ Part Two $16.95
\_\_\_\_\_ Blackhawk $16.95
\_\_\_\_\_ Batman $16.95
\_\_\_\_\_ The UNCLE Technical Manual One $9.95 \_\_\_\_\_ Two $9.95
\_\_\_\_\_ The Green Hornet Television Book $14.95
\_\_\_\_\_ Number Six The Prisoner Book $14.95
\_\_\_\_\_ The Wild Wild West $17.95
\_\_\_\_\_ Trek Year One $10.95
\_\_\_\_\_ Trek Year Two $12.95
\_\_\_\_\_ Trek Year Three $12.95
\_\_\_\_\_ The Animated Trek $14.95
\_\_\_\_\_ The Movies $12.95
\_\_\_\_\_ Next Generation $19.95
\_\_\_\_\_ The Lost Years $14.95
\_\_\_\_\_ The Trek Encyclopedia $19.95
\_\_\_\_\_ Interviews Aboard The Enterprise $18.95
\_\_\_\_\_ The Ultimate Trek $75.00
\_\_\_\_\_ Trek Handbook $12.95 \_\_\_\_\_ Trek Universe $17.95
\_\_\_\_\_ The Crew Book $17.95
\_\_\_\_\_ The Making of the Next Generation $14.95
\_\_\_\_\_ The Freddy Krueger Story $14.95
\_\_\_\_\_ The Aliens Story $14.95
\_\_\_\_\_ Robocop $16.95
\_\_\_\_\_ Monsterland's Horror in the '80s $17.95
\_\_\_\_\_ The Compleat Lost in Space $17.95
\_\_\_\_\_ Lost in Space Tribute Book $9.95
\_\_\_\_\_ Lost in Space Tech Manual $9.95
\_\_\_\_\_ Supermarionation $17.95
\_\_\_\_\_ The Unofficial Beauty and the Beast $14.95
\_\_\_\_\_ Dark Shadows Tribute Book $14.95
\_\_\_\_\_ Dark Shadows Interview Book $18.95
\_\_\_\_\_ Doctor Who Baker Years $19.95
\_\_\_\_\_ The Doctor Who Encyclopedia: The 4th Doctor $19.95
\_\_\_\_\_ Illustrated Stephen King $12.95
\_\_\_\_\_ Gunsmoke Years $14.95

NAME: _____

STREET: _____

CITY: _____

STATE: _____

ZIP: _____

TOTAL: _____ SHIPPING _____

SEND TO: COUCH POTATO, INC.
5715 N BALSAM, LAS VEGAS, NV 89130

# EXCITING EARLY ISSUES!

If your local comic book specialty store no longer has copies of the early issues you may want to order them directly from us.

**By Roy Crane:**
_Buz Sawyer #1 _Buz Sawyer #2 _Buz Sawyer #3 _Buz Sawyer #4 _Buz Sawyer #5

**By Alex Raymond:**
_Jungle Jim 1 _Jungle Jim 2 _Jungle Jim 3 _Jungle Jim 4 _Jungle Jim 5 _Jungle Jim 6 _Jungle Jim 7
_Rip Kirby #1 _Rip Kirby #2 _Rip Kirby #3 _Rip Kirby #4

**By Lee Falk and Phil Davis:**
_Mandrake #1 _Mandrake #2 _Mandrake #3 _Mandrake #4 _Mandrake #5 _Mandrake #6 _Mandrake #7

**By Peter O'Donnell and Jim Holdaway:**
_Modesty 1 _Modesty 2 _Modesty 3 _Modesty 4 _Modesty 5 _Modesty #6 _Modesty #7
_Modesty ANNUAL ($5.00)

**By Hal Foster:**
_P V #1 _P V #2 _P V #3 _P V #4 _P V #5 _P V #6 _P V #7 _P V #8 _P V AN. ($5.00)

**By Archie Goodwin and Al Williamson:**
_Secret Agent #1 _Secret Agent #2 _Secret Agent #3 _Secret Agent #4 _Secret Agent #5 _Secret Agent #6

(All about the heroes including interviews with Hal Foster, Lee Falk and Al Williamson:)
___ THE KING COMIC HEROES   $14.95
(The following two book-size collections preserve the original strip format)
___ THE MANDRAKE SUNDAYS   $14.95
___ **THE PHANTOM SUNDAYS**   $14.95

___ (Enclosed) Please enclose $3.00 per comic ordered
and/or $17.95 for THE KING COMIC HEROES
and/or $14.95 for THE MANDRAKE SUNDAYS.
and/or $14.95 for THE PHANTOM SUNDAYS.
Shipping and handling are included.

Name: _____

Street: _____

City: _____

State: _____

Zip Code: _____

**Check or money order only.** No cash please. All payments must be in US funds. Please add $5.00 to foreign orders.
**I remembered to enclose:**$____
Please send to:
Pioneer, 5715 N. Balsam Rd., Las Vegas, NV 89130